Gloria Pa.



Book "Silence" Robert Ad

when you take yourself seriously you know the ego is involved.

**Releasing Guilt for Inner Peace**

*A companion to 4 Habits for Inner Peace*

disruptive - secretary

By

Elizabeth Cronkhite

God is pure awareness & stillness. No subject/object just subject "Awareness." H.P.

"Journey through the workbook"

- who am I? Who are these thoughts coming to. Whom which
- Am I my thoughts
- Am I my Body. No I am pure awareness
- I'm not my thoughts
- I'm not my body.

"I am that I am"

*All of the examples in this book were made up by the author and are deliberately generic. Any resemblance to persons living or dead is coincidental.*

**Other Books by Liz Cronkhite**

The ACIM Mentor Articles

The Plain Language A Course in Miracles:
*The Message of A Course in Miracles* (Text)
*Practicing A Course in Miracles/The Way of A Course in Miracles* (Workbook/Manual for Teachers)

4 Habits for Inner Peace

## Contents

## Introduction

The only way to inner peace is through an awareness of the Truth within you. In *4 Habits for Inner Peace* you learned that as you turn your mind inward to Truth you encounter your obstacles to peace: guilt and the fear that it inspires. So the way to inner peace is through two intersecting processes. You invite Truth into your awareness by practicing the four habits. This brings up your unconscious and conscious beliefs in guilt. Then with the Teacher of Truth in your mind you look at and release your belief in guilt. This brings Truth back into your awareness. Your awareness of Truth grows faster as you release guilt.

In this book, a companion to *4HIP*, you will look closely at guilt. You will learn where guilt comes from, how it is maintained in your mind, how to recognize it, and how to release it to be at peace. You will see how the personal thought system uses smoke (denial) and mirrors (projections) to maintain guilt in your mind. You will see how it contradicts itself. You will see how guilt has no basis. And this will help you to release guilt.

The personal thought system in your mind will be very resistant to you examining guilt. And your belief in guilt will make you accept its resistance as your own. So fear may manifest for you as you read this book. You may feel anxious or have moments of down-right panic. You may have bouts of cognitive disorientation and physical dizziness. You may feel as though you and/or the author have fallen down the rabbit hole. You may have thoughts that you are killing yourself with the ideas in this book. Your body may get ill. Any of these may occur when you are reading or when you are going about your day not consciously thinking about what this book says. Or your mind's resistance may be so strong that you will not be able to understand what you read.

If your discomfort reading this book is overwhelming or if you cannot understand it at all guilt is still too real to you. You may want to read the last part, *Releasing Guilt*, first so that you learn about the benefits of releasing guilt. Then come back to this book later when you have grown your awareness of Truth enough to know that the Truth *is* True. Only then will you be able to look at guilt with some detachment.

If you can recognize the personal thought system's forms of resistance as what they are and let them pass then you are ready to examine guilt. You will recognize the forms that guilt takes long before you will release guilt. But acknowledging and recognizing guilt are the necessary first steps to releasing it. You will know that you have begun to release guilt when you look on the personal thought system in yourself and in others without judgment. You will see that they are nothing.

## Guilt and God

1. What guilt is and how it shows up

Guilt is a deep-seated feeling of "I am wrong" or "I am bad"; or "I have done something wrong" or "I have done something bad".

All feelings and all behaviors are effects of conscious or unconscious thoughts. So feelings of guilt and the behaviors to which they lead you originate in conscious and/or unconscious beliefs that you are wrong or bad or that you have done something wrong or bad.

Some ways that a belief in guilt shows up are fear of a god, expectation of punishment, generalized unworthiness, generalized inadequacy, self-loathing, judging yourself, judging others, thinking that others are judging you, taking others' attitudes and behaviors personally, confusing responsibility with blame, defensiveness, secretiveness, dishonesty, generalized anxiety, generalized fear, generalized anger, martyrdom, perfectionism, being hard on yourself, self-medicating with a substance or behavior, an inability to be alone, an inability to tolerate quiet, an inability to meditate, an inability to be present, busy-ness, nightmares, worry and anxiety about the future, worry and anxiety about loved ones, thoughts and images of you or loved ones or strangers being tortured, the need to be right, the need to win, over-achieving, the need to fix others, the need to fix the world, sacrificing, co-dependency, fear of success, fear of good outcomes for you, masochism, self-destructive behavior, self-sabotage, interpreting neutral events (natural disaster, disease, etc.) as punishment or proof of guilt, interpreting others' behavior as punishment or proof of *your* guilt, and spiritualizing the self. Examples of many of these responses are given throughout this book.

Physical illnesses may manifest a belief in guilt. You may unconsciously hurt yourself, make yourself ill, or ignore physical symptoms to punish yourself for your guilt.

*Rosa chronically bruises herself, pulls muscles, and breaks bones. Unconsciously she is punishing herself for what she sees as her inherent sinfulness.*

*Tristan has an auto-immune disease that he manages well except when he feels he has done something wrong. Then to punish himself he unconsciously chooses to push himself to physical exhaustion and to eat foods that he knows exacerbate his condition.*

*Sita ignores the lump under her arm because she unconsciously believes that she deserves to get cancer and die.*

Certainly interpreting illness as proof of guilt or as punishment means you believe guilt is real.

*Lola went to the doctor with symptoms that she felt certain meant she had a serious illness. When the doctor confirmed this she was not surprised. She always knew she was guilty and would be punished one day with some horrible disease.*

Certain mental illnesses exaggerate guilt. And any mental illness is exacerbated by guilt.

*Like everyone, Waldo unconsciously believes he is guilty. But his mental illness makes him see threats everywhere. He unconsciously expects to be punished.*

*Eva is a narcissist who is unable to take responsibility for anything. She blames anyone around her for anything that goes wrong. Even her small mistakes threaten to make her aware of the huge guilt she unconsciously feels.*

*Alfonso washes his hands obsessively because he feels inherently dirty (guilty). His obsessive-compulsive symptoms are worse when he feels he has done something wrong.*

*Sandy's depression worsened when she realized that she let her friend down by not showing up at her party.*

Guilt is in every mind in the personal thought system. But a chemical imbalance can make you have thoughts and feelings of guilt that you would not have otherwise. If this is the case then medication is necessary to bring you back into balance. Then you can deal with your underlying belief in guilt rather than be distracted by its symptoms.

You may think that you do not believe in guilt. You may think that you do not feel guilt. The personal thought system is very good at keeping guilt out of your conscious awareness. But you can see by the list in the third paragraph above how when you identify as a self guilt pervades your responses to and interactions with the world. If you have any of these responses at any time, you unconsciously or consciously believe in guilt and experience guilt.

## 2. Guilt and social conscience

In your identification with a self you feel guilt at least sometimes. You may feel guilt much or all of the time. You may point to past behavior or events as sources for your guilt. You may point to personal character flaws as sources for your guilt. You may feel generalized guilt, which is guilt that does not seem to have a specific source.

When you are very young adults are supposed to teach you the boundaries and laws of your family, culture, and society. These rules of right and wrong form a *social-morality*. As you learn these you develop a *social conscience*. Your social conscience is an internal sense of what is right or wrong according to your family, culture, or society. It is what feels disturbed when you violate social-morality. Rules, boundaries, and laws vary among families, cultures, and societies. They also change over time as values change and more is learned about the world and human nature. Though arbitrary, social-morality is a starting point for living in relative harmony with others in the world.

When rational and realistic, rules, boundaries, and laws serve the well-being of a family, culture, or society. But the belief in an *absolute-morality* results in unrealistic and/or harsh social-moralities to control members of a family, culture, or society. Absolute-morality, if it existed, would be right and wrong behavior in the world as decreed by a power, or god, over it. Your unconscious belief in absolute-morality is your belief that guilt is an intrinsic aspect of reality. When you confuse absolute-morality and social-morality, social-morality becomes an attempt to control what is seen as *intrinsic guilt*.

A disturbed social conscience and feeling guilty are not the same experience. But the personal thought system hijacks your social conscience to "prove" your guilt. A social conscience refers to the self's behavior in the world in relation to others. If guilt does not become involved with it, your social conscience is assuaged through amends or a genuine change in values. Guilt, however, is the feeling that the imperfect and sometimes mistaken self is proof that you are *intrinsically* wrong or bad. Guilt cannot be swept away. Where your social conscience sees temporary mistakes easily corrected, your belief in intrinsic guilt sees eternal sins that can never be undone. It twists your social conscience into a useful source for guilt.

*Alice stepped on Peter's toe. She could not undo the toe-stepping and did not have access to ice for the sore toe so she offered "I'm sorry" as amends to Peter. Peter laughed and accepted her apology for the common, every-day occurrence. If guilt were not involved Alice would accept that as a person she is not perfect and that she makes mistake. She made what amends she could and she could just let it go. But because of unconscious guilt in her mind she feels disproportionately bad about the incident. Peter has accepted her apology, but nothing that she offers as amends feels like enough to her. Later, she replays the incident in her mind over and over in cringing embarrassment. It has become another example of how inherently imperfect she is.*

*Guido goes to the other extreme and is defensive when he rear-ends Barbara's car. She braked suddenly to avoid hitting a car that had stopped short in front of her. She had left enough space between her car and that car so that she could brake suddenly, just as happened. But Guido was following too closely behind Barbara and hit her. He rages and blames Barbara for his mistake. He makes himself the victim and blames her for the accident. He blames an unjust society for the ticket he gets for the accident. If he did not feel unconscious guilt he would just apologize, pay the ticket, and learn from this situation to keep a safe distance behind cars in front of him in the future. But guilt turns his simple mistake into defensive rage. His thoughts and words can lie, but his feelings do not. His feelings of defensiveness, his need to justify, and his anger at others indicate that he feels guilty. In fact, he feels so overwhelmed by guilt that he cannot admit a small human error. A small admission of guilt threatens to make him aware of the mountain of guilt he believes is within him. Later that day he gets stoned to repress the social conscience that nearly brought all of his guilt to his conscious awareness.*

*Barney committed a small crime. His social conscience could be swept clean by "paying his debt to society" through time in jail, community service, or prison. But a deep belief in his mind that he is bad (guilty) twists his behavioral errors into proof of his intrinsic sinfulness. After some community service he commits another crime. Over the years, though given many chances, he always falls back into a life of crime. He thinks that his behavior proves that he is bad. But really his behavior only acts out his belief that he is bad.*

*Tony feels that it is against his nature to be sexually exclusive with one partner. Monogamous marriage feels inauthentic and unrealistic for him. By choosing to not marry he violates his family's and religion's requirement of monogamous marriage in adulthood. Because his values are now based on an honest assessment of his nature, his social conscience could be at ease. Guilt, however, drives him to avoid his family. Their pressure on him to marry mirrors his own internal pressure to conform. Deep down he feels that he is wrong to go against his religion's edicts.*

The belief in intrinsic guilt can result in maintaining a social-morality that is based in ignorance. If a family, culture, or society believes that their values represent absolute-morality then they are afraid to change them. So they will fight against or at least deny facts that show those values to be based in ignorance.

*Winona is white. She was raised in a religion that taught her to obey her parents. Her parents physically, psychologically, and emotionally enforced obedience to them. They also taught her to fear and hate people with dark skin. But in college her experience of dark-skinned people has taught her that they are just people with a different skin color. She's learned that skin color does not determine humanness or intelligence or reveal character. So she has learned that her family's fear of others with dark skin is based in ignorance.*

*Because her values are now based in fact, her social conscience is not disturbed by her knowing that skin color is only a superficial human trait. But she feels a deep-seated fear that going against her parent's wishes is a "sin" against her god. So she continues to avoid dark-skinned people.*

You need a social conscience to navigate the self through the world. But you do not need guilt. It is only an obstacle to peace.

3. Guilt without a social conscience

As the opposite of Oneness, or Infinite Sameness, not-Truth expresses itself through diversity along a spectrum. The content of all personal thought systems is the same – not-True – and they are expressed as variations on the same themes:

*Casey is clinically narcissistic.*

*Caroline takes everything personally.*

*Hugo can be self-centered sometimes.*

And at any given moment their traits are expressed to different degrees:

*Luis is anxious at this moment.*

*Brett is terrified at this moment.*

*Frances' fears are unconscious for the moment.*

Social consciences also develop along a spectrum and are expressed to varying degrees. Three to four percent of people do not even have a social conscience. In the world they are commonly called *sociopaths*.

There is argument in the world over whether sociopaths have a disorder (Antisocial Personality Disorder) that develops or are simply a personality type that has naturally evolved. In any case, sociopaths exemplify a personal thought system unfettered by a social conscience. They exist only for themselves. They cannot feel empathy for others. They do not feel remorse when they violate social-morals. They relate to others only to get something from them. They enjoy manipulating and sometimes even destroying others. They do not take responsibility for their own actions. They are paranoid, secretive, grandiose, and superficially charming to get what they want. But while they do not have a social conscience to be hijacked by guilt, they manifest an unconscious belief in intrinsic guilt.

A sociopath may be conscious of superficial fears related to their survival and to their freedom. They do not want to die or to be imprisoned. But psychologists report a deep rage at the center of a sociopath's personality. Anger in any form, from mild irritation to rage, is a defensive posture. And defensiveness indicates fear. All fear is really a fear of punishment for guilt. So anger and fear always reveal an unconscious or conscious belief in intrinsic guilt. (This is elaborated on in part 7).

Sociopaths also fear being exposed as essentially empty within. This is not a fear of being socially rejected, because they are good at avoiding this through manipulation. This is an expression of their unconscious belief that they are lacking, imperfect, wrong, and/or bad. They unconsciously believe in intrinsic guilt.

Guilt is the universal experience of a self. You do not need a social conscience to experience guilt.

## 4. Why there is guilt in your mind

To understand why there is guilt in your mind you must understand how your experience of a self in a body in a world is out of accord with Reality, or Truth.

Truth is formless Being extending without limit. It is an experience of boundless love, peace, and joy. Truth is All that is. Being All that is, Truth must contain the idea of Its Own opposite. But since Truth is All that is, It cannot have an actual opposite. So the opposite-of-Truth, or not-Truth, is only ever an idea.

Like Truth, the idea of not-Truth simply *is*. It only arises because Truth must think of Its Own opposite. But the All-encompassing nature of Truth undoes the idea of Its Own opposite as soon as it is thought. So not-Truth has no intention, no purpose, and no meaning. It has no reality. It has not happened.

But *within the idea* of not-Truth, not-Truth seems to have intention, purpose, and meaning. It seems to be a replacement reality for Reality. It seems to have "killed" Truth. Since Truth is formless, eternal, and infinite, the idea of not-Truth is projected as a universe of time-bound limited form. Only your belief in the story for time makes not-Truth seem real to you. In Truth the idea of not-Truth is already undone.

Mind is the aspect of Being through which Being knows Itself. The part of Mind in which the idea of not-Truth seems to occur seems to be split off from Truth. But it is never actually split off from Truth. Truth is still there beyond the idea of not-Truth. So within itself this part of Mind is actually split between Truth and not-Truth. Truth merely is. And not-Truth actively denies Truth. This is the conflict of the split-mind.

Since Truth is One, or the same throughout, the split-mind, being the opposite of Truth, projects itself into the universe of form as billions of diverse versions of itself. These take the forms of seemingly-unique split-minds in unique bodies, or *selves*. Not-Truth in each individual mind takes the form of a *personal thought system.* The sole purpose of the personal thought system is to deny the Truth in the individual mind and to perpetuate not-Truth (including itself) as reality. It has no positive goal for the individual mind. It is only concerned with its own seeming-existence, which means to remain in its individual mind's awareness.

What you think of as you is one of these projections of the conflicted split-mind. You seem to be born in a body in a world with a personal thought system already in your mind. It speaks for you as a self in a world. And since this is what you think is reality you accept what it says without question until you maybe one day do question it. (And you have so you are reading this). Truth is always in your mind, too, beyond the personal thought system. But It comes into your awareness only when you choose for It to do so, unconsciously or consciously. Truth cannot rise to your conscious awareness without your invitation because your belief in the self as your reality blocks Its way.

The personal thought system believes, mistakenly, that it is real. So it believes, mistakenly, that it has killed Truth. But it also senses a Power greater than it within you. And it believes, correctly, that it opposes this Power. It means to kill this Power and empower itself. (Yes, these are conflicting beliefs: its existence proves that it killed Truth and it must also still kill Truth to claim Its power. This is discussed further in the next part).

In your identification with a self you believe, consciously and mistakenly, that the self is real and that it is you. So you believe, unconsciously and mistakenly, that *you* have killed Truth. You believe, unconsciously or consciously, but mistakenly, that you oppose a Power greater than yourself.

You unconsciously accept the absurd idea that you killed (and somehow also now oppose) Truth because in your identification with a self you feel that something is "wrong". What is "wrong" is that you are not in your natural limitless state. But in your identification with a thought system that thinks that it exists because it killed Truth your feeling that "something is wrong" is interpreted as "I am wrong because I killed Truth". So there is guilt in your mind because you incorrectly interpret your discomfort identifying with a limited self as intrinsic wrongness for killing Truth. Guilt is a made-up concept. It has no reality. You feel guilty for something that has not occurred and can never occur.

You cannot penetrate through guilt from the personal thought system because guilt and the personal thought system form a closed circle. Your identification with it is the source of your guilt. And your guilt implies that it is real. To the personal thought system its existence and your guilt are one and the same.

The value of guilt for the personal thought system does not end with its validation. Guilt binds its power source to it through fear, ensuring its continuance. And its power source is you.

5. Giving away your Power and accepting guilt

Reality cannot oppose itself. So either limitless, formless Being or a limited universe of form is reality. This is why if you believe that the self is your reality you also must believe that Truth does not exist. But It does and It is eternal and It is within you. And on some level you know this. So your disbelief in It is really just denial.

The reason that you easily accept unconscious guilt is that when you identify with a self you and the personal thought system have similar stories. You deny your Power (Truth) by identifying with a limited self. And the personal thought system seeks to destroy your Power. As far as feeling guilty is concerned, denying Truth and destroying It are not all that different.

The personal thought system cannot actually destroy you because without you it cannot seem to exist. It is a thought system in your mind that only has seeming-existence when you give it your attention. Yet it is out to kill What (Truth) is real in you. So the personal thought system knows that its seeming-existence is very precarious. This is why it is inherently insecure and defensive. To believe in its own reality it must believe that it killed Truth. But its power source (you) is a mind that is part of the Mind of Truth. Your mind may seem to be split off from the Mind of Truth but this is not actually so. So the personal thought system knows that there is Something Else in the mind of its power source to Which it is opposed. Since it opposes this Something Else it feels opposed by It. (Although Truth does not oppose the personal thought system. Truth does not know of not-Truth because not-Truth is not real). So deep down within itself the personal thought system knows that it has not succeeded in killing off Truth. And if it has not succeeded in killing off Truth it does not really exist.

Truth and not-Truth are diametrically opposed so they cannot know or understand each other. The personal thought system does not understand the Truth in your mind. As you grow your awareness of Truth it only knows that sometimes your attention goes to Something that it cannot understand. It is powerless. It has no power over you. It is only an idea that does not seem to exist for you until you give your attention to it. This is why, as soon as you turn your attention back to it even a little bit, it will attack you in some way to hold your attention. It will fill your mind with doubt, insecurity, dark thoughts, memories, desires, etc. It does not care if you love it or hate it. It only needs your belief in it to be empowered.

The personal thought system experiences your split-mind, its source, in two ways. One is as its power source, which it knows how to manipulate to preserve itself. It does this with guilt. This built-in validator also protects it. Guilt makes you fear to look inward because you believe that you will see how horrible you really are. And as long as you do not look inward you will not find Truth and learn that the personal thought system is not your reality.

The other way that the personal thought system experiences your mind is with a Power within you that is outside of it. It incorrectly assumes that this Power wants to punish it. The personal thought system believes this because it can only understand itself. It punishes so it assumes that this unknowable Power outside of it punishes, too.

When you identify with a self you unconsciously fear the Power (Truth) within you as though it is a power, or god, over and outside of you that intends to punish you for your guilt. In other words, when you identify with a self the god that you fear is you. You literally fear yourself.

But there is no god outside of you. There is no power over you. The Truth is the Power *within* you.

6. Anger as fear of punishment

Anger is a defensive response to a perceived threat. So anger in any form, from mild irritation to rage, indicates unconscious fear.

*Gilda jumped back in surprise when she saw the cockroach. This was an instinctive response. But then she angrily wacked it into pulp with her shoe because she was afraid of it.*

*Darien felt a twinge of irritation when his wife brought up her old boyfriend again. He was unconsciously afraid that she loved her ex more than him.*

*With his monster truck Spuds rammed the back of the car that he perceived cut him off. The driver of the other car represented to Spuds's subconscious everyone whom he ever felt took his power. He was overcome by rage.*

Behind all fear is guilt. You would not feel fear if you did not identify with a self. Certainly the self is limited and its body is vulnerable and these are frightening in themselves. But your identification with a self is the source of your guilt. And your real fear is fear of punishment from a power over you. Fears that you cannot trace back to fear of punishment are fears that reinforce your fear of punishment. In the examples above each experienced fear for the self because they believed that the self was their reality. This unconsciously reinforced for each guilt and fear of punishment from a power over them.

If you consciously believe in a god then you think that it is the power over you that will punish you for your guilt. If you do not consciously believe in a god you fear punishment but you do not define what is supposed to punish you.

*Muriel's city recently passed legislation that Muriel feels is sinful. When the hurricane destroyed much of her city, including her home, she was sure it was punishment from her god. Even though she didn't support the legislation she also did nothing to stop it.*

*Dusty was planning a very elaborate wedding. She unconsciously felt guilty for this extravagance. Then her beloved grandmother died suddenly a week before the wedding. Now Dusty feels that she is being punished. She does not consciously believe in a punishing god. But she also does not ask herself what is punishing her.*

In these examples each interpreted natural events as punishment because they believed that their guilt was real. But you may also unconsciously punish yourself in the hope that you will mitigate future punishment from a power outside of you.

*Julie left her husband and children. Living with them was too stressful. But in her guilt she will never allow herself to be happy in her new life. She feels that she should suffer for her sin. She hopes that if she suffers now her god won't punish her later.*

Since punishment is supposed to be a god's prerogative, punishing yourself to mitigate his punishment of you is a grab at his power. So punishing yourself unconsciously *increases* your guilt.

Guilt can make you feel unworthy of good. So when what you judge as good comes to you, you fear that you will be punished for accepting what you do not deserve.

*Things were going very well in every aspect of Kyle's life. But his unconscious guilt made him fear that he did not deserve it. So he unconsciously made a mistake while driving and totaled his car. He sustained critical injuries.*

*Angie has a pattern in her business life of great successes followed by huge failures. She has fantastic business acumen that leads to easy successes. But unconsciously she feels that she does not deserve success. So she unconsciously sabotages her businesses and fails each time.*

Guilt demands that you "earn" what is judged as good. If you do not earn it then you should "pay" for it afterward.

*Anson's first book was an instant best seller worldwide. He became wealthy off of it. His quick success is very rare for a writer and he unconsciously feels that he does not deserve it. So he does not manage his money well. He gives it away and spends it quickly.*

You may feel guilty for undeserved "gifts" for which you are not responsible.

*Kera is incredibly bright. She realized at a very young age that she had intellectual gifts that far outstripped her classmates. Her parents and teachers did not want her to become egotistical so they taught her that her intellectual gifts meant that she bore greater responsibility than others. Through the guilt in her mind she unconsciously interpreted this to mean that she had an absolute-moral obligation to fix the world. She became a leader but at great price to her peace of mind. She is driven to fix the world and she is crushed by guilt when she fails.*

Anxiety and worry about the future are really expectation of punishment. They reveal that you feel guilty. And in practice they are a form of present self-punishment for guilt.

*Although Kareem makes a good living and manages his money well he often imagines scenarios of future personal financial disaster. He unconsciously expects things to go wrong as punishment for his intrinsic guilt. But his feelings of anxiety punish him now.*

*Chrystal worries constantly about her children even though they are adults who have moved away. She unconsciously expects to lose a child as punishment for her intrinsic guilt. But she suffers now as she thinks about possible future loss.*

Fear of punishment sometimes manifests through horrifying images in your mind. They are a form of present torture under the guise of a fear of possible torture. Sometimes these images are fleeting. Sometimes you may obsess on them to punish yourself now.

*Chase has noticed that since he has become aware of Truth terrible images of mutilation or torture will sometimes cross through his mind. He recognizes that this is just his belief in guilt manifesting. He does not dwell on the thoughts. He lets them pass. But he acknowledges the guilt so that he does not unconsciously do something to harm himself. Then he turns his mind inward to Truth and remembers that guilt is not real.*

*Since hearing about the practice of genital mutilation in Africa, Sylvia has not been able to stop thinking about it. It fills her with horror that this happens to others. She feels a dread that this could ever happen to her. Her thoughts torture her. She cannot stop thinking about this because unconsciously she feels that she deserves punishment for her intrinsic guilt.*

7. Denying your belief in a punishing god

You may think that you are an atheist and do not believe in a god. Or you may think that you believe in a god but not one that punishes. If so, look back to the third paragraph in part 1 and see if you ever respond to the world in the ways listed there. If you do not then you have released all of the guilt in your mind. How blessed you are to be wholly at peace! Rejoice that the world will soon fall from your mind and only boundless Truth will remain!

But if you do at least sometimes respond in some of the ways listed there then you believe in guilt. And if you believe in guilt you must believe in *something* with power over you that you have defied and that will punish you, even if your belief is only unconscious and never labeled “god”. You fear this punishing something, unconsciously or consciously, or you would easily release guilt.

*Albert is an atheist from a family of atheists and agnostics. He says that he believes in only what the senses of his body report to him or in what math can prove to him.*

*But Albert is a perfectionist. He must do everything according to the standards he has set for himself or he feels deep anxiety. He says that he just has high standards for himself. But actually he feels deeply afraid that he will be punished if he is not perfect. He is unconsciously trying to atone for intrinsic guilt that he unconsciously believes is real.*

*Even if Albert could be brought to acknowledge his guilt he still would not be able to say toward what he feels guilty. But he unconsciously feels that he must be perfect to appease a punishing god.*

If you manifest guilt but think that you do not believe in a *punishing* god it is because you feel guilty for believing that your god punishes. So you deny that you believe in a punishing god despite feelings that show that you do.

*Cleo has attended a liberal New Thought church most of her adult life. Her god is a loving god. She says she loves God; she does not fear God. In fact she thinks that people who fear God are foolish and do not know God.*

*Cleo bases her personal and political views on what she believes her god wants for the world. And she feels that people who hold personal and political views different from hers are wrong and sometimes even "evil". She never stops to think about whose rules or laws they seem to violate to make her react so strongly. She does not know that she sees the unconscious guilt in her own mind reflected in the guilt that she sees in others. And she unconsciously fears that, just like those others, she will be punished by her god for her guilt.*

Everyone is born into the world with a personal thought system in their mind. So no matter what one may claim to believe, guilt, fear, and a sense of a punishing power over them are in their mind. Ironically, universal unconscious guilt reveals a universal unconscious awareness of Truth. Even though the Power (Truth) within is unconsciously misunderstood as a power over, there would be no guilt at all without an awareness that Something is being denied.

You can lie about what you think but feelings do not lie. They are caused by your real thoughts, no matter what you say to yourself or to others. You can repress feelings, keep yourself busy to avoid them, or self-medicate to numb yourself against them. But feelings will manifest what you really believe, whether you choose to pay attention to them or not. Only if you choose to acknowledge the guilt that shows up in your feelings and behavior will you be able to release your belief in guilt.

8. The jumble god of not-Truth, Truth, and you

If you want to release guilt to be aware of Truth and be at peace you must untangle your experiences of Truth from the concept of a god that is central to maintaining guilt in your mind. It is vital to the personal thought system's preservation that you confuse the two.

*Charlotte had a strong religious upbringing. She has also experienced the boundless love and peace of Truth, which she calls "God". These experiences draw her further into her religion and make her trust it. But much of her church's doctrine and dogma seems to contradict her loving experiences of Truth. She cannot reconcile the church's guilt and fear with the True Love that she has experienced. So she just doesn't think about it. She stays with her church because she fears that questioning it is a sin. But her confusion limits how open she is to experiencing Truth again. So it limits how much peace she experiences.*

The personal thought system is aware that it did not make itself. Its maker is the split-mind, which projects it as part of the idea of not-Truth. And it is aware of a Power (Truth) outside of it that is within the power (you) over it. So the personal thought system responds to several things it does not understand as though they are all part of one god: its maker (the split-mind), Truth (a Power outside of it), and you (the individual mind that empowers it). But it can understand itself and only itself. So it thinks its god is like itself: insecure, defensive, punishing, inconsistent, capricious, and arbitrary. It thinks of its god as just a greater self. (And here at the beginning of the 21st century, still usually a *male* self). But because the personal thought system knows that it did not make itself it thinks that it is made in the image of this god.

Despite its belief in a power over it, in practice the personal thought system only serves itself. And its concept of a god only serves it. So while in theory it holds up the idea of a god outside of itself, in practice it worships and serves only itself.

You are unconsciously aware of a Power that you deny. This Power is within you. But in your identification with a self It seems outside of you and over you. So you unconsciously accept It as the personal thought system's jumble-god made of the split-mind, Truth, and you shrouded in a projection of the personal thought system's traits. And you fear to look inward not just because of the guilt that is blocking your way to Truth. You also fear the Truth within you because you unconsciously equate It with this capricious, punishing jumble-god.

So if you want to release guilt you need to look at and question the existence of the god that upholds guilt in your mind.

9. Undoing the projected god

Some of not-Truth's religions openly require that to belong you declare your guilt ("I am a sinner…") before you can accept their god ("…and I accept Jesus Christ as my savior…") with even more guilt ("… because *He* died for *my* sins."). Not-Truth's religions do not cause their followers to feel guilt and fear. They only give overt expression to a universal experience of guilt. Their founders had guilt in their minds and they believed in it. Rather than question the guilt they sought to explain it with concepts such as "original sin". People are attracted to religion because it validates the guilt in their mind that they unconsciously or consciously believe to be true.

*Concita did not have a religious upbringing. But she had insecure parents who put her down and often made her their scapegoat. This gave shape to the guilt that was already in the personal thought system in her mind. As an adult she has not addressed this and she continues to have low self-esteem. A Christian friend invited her to church one Sunday. The pastor gave a sermon on intrinsic sinfulness and the need to humbly admit your sinfulness to be accepted by their god. Concita left the church with a feeling of relief. The pastor had confirmed for her what she had always felt: she is intrinsically bad. The next week she joined the church.*

For obvious reasons the two greatest sins that you can commit from the personal thought system's point of view are to question your guilt and to question its god. But these are what you must do if you want to release guilt and be at peace.

Even if you are not religious unconscious guilt and the concept of a god that upholds guilt in your mind are central to your personal thought system. So you may feel overtly fearful as you read this section and question the existence of a god. Recognize that this is the personal thought system's defenses kicking in. The fear of god that you seem to feel is your belief in guilt. And the fear of death that you seem to feel is the personal thought system's fear of being released.

There is a Power greater than the self but It is not a god. In this book It is called *Truth*. Truth is an experience within you of limitless love, peace, and joy. It is an experience of wholeness unlike anything the personal experience has to offer. To experience Truth is to *know* It. "God" is a concept of a personified power over you that you cannot experience because it is only an idea. You may have anticipated punishment from a god. You may have punished yourself in the hope that a god would punish you less. You may have interpreted events as punishment from a god. You may have thought that the experience of Truth came from a god. But you have never directly experienced a god. You have only *believed in* a god.

The Truth within you is untouched by your belief in a god. It is not affected in any way by your perception of not-Truth as reality. When you experience Truth you experience true forgiveness, or release, of the idea that guilt is real. Every time that you let Truth into your awareness in any way you detach from the self and guilt a little more.

Truth is unchanging and unchangeable. Your acceptance of not-Truth as reality only affects you in your belief that you are not-True, or a self. But the Truth is always in your mind, too. Since It is Love your awareness of It shows up not as punishment but as correction. When you allow It into your awareness It manifests in your seemingly-individual mind as a thought system to replace the personal thought system. This thought system is your *Teacher of*

*Truth* because It leads your mind back to its natural wholeness in Truth. When the self seems like your reality the Teacher of Truth seems like Something within you to guide and advise you. It feels "other". In time, as your trust in It grows, It becomes your Constant Companion as you go about the world. Then the line between you and It blurs and It is your thought system as you release the personal thought system. Finally, the personal thought system, the self, the world, and the Teacher of Truth fall away from your mind and only Truth remains.

Unlike your awareness of Truth your belief in a god does not cause a shift in you. It maintains guilt and fear in your mind. It does not bring release of any kind. And it is affected by your awareness of Truth: it falls away.

When you openly believe in a god the personal thought system tells you that he is all-powerful. It must to make you fear him. And it must also tell you that "God is Love" because it knows that you will not accept unmitigated fear. But look at these ideas:

You are supposed to have denied, attacked, killed, or somehow hurt God. So God must punish you. But if He were truly all-powerful, like Truth, He could not be harmed, affected, or changed in any way. In fact this god is so insecure and sensitive that you cannot even question His existence without fear of punishment! This god is not all-powerful.

Look closer: If God is defensive then God must be insecure. If God attacks or punishes He must feel that He needs to demonstrate His strength. So He must feel weak. If God is judgmental then he projects guilt. So He must feel guilty. If God is capricious, arbitrary, and inconsistent then He must be incomplete and unstable. Does this sound like something all-powerful? It sounds like the personal thought system of which it is a projection! If this god existed he would be frightening because he is so unstable. But he is only an idea meant to hold guilt in your mind.

Now look at fear and Love together: Fear, a manifestation of your belief in not-Truth, and Love, the experience of Truth, are diametrically opposed. Fear is caused by a belief in lack. Love is the experience of Wholeness. Fear and Love cannot be reconciled. So if you believe in its god, the personal thought system tells you to accept "on faith" that its frightening god is also Love. But it cannot give you any proof of this. In fact, its god is supposed to have made a universe of lack and limitation which he populated with people made in his image. He then set them up to defy him. And when they did he punished them and all who came after with painful, limited existences. Is this Love? Love does not set you up to fail and then punish you when you do. Those are the actions of a petty tyrant who needs to play power games to feel powerful. You may believe that a god made the world. You may believe that God is Love. But you cannot honestly believe that both are true about the same god.

When you find that you fear punishment ask yourself what there is to punish you. There is no power outside of you. Truth is the Power within you. And It is Love, not fear. Think about the weak, vulnerable god that makes no sense but that the personal thought system tells you to fear. *Question its existence.* Then remember your *experiences* of Truth.

You will release your belief in a god outside of you with power over you when you realize that it is just a concept. And if there is no god whom you have offended there is no basis for guilt. There is nothing to fear.

## Guilt and the Self

10. The self and fear of Truth

You seemed to be born into a body in a world. You seem to have a thought system in your mind which identifies with the body. The body and the personal thought system make up a self which you believe is reality unless you become aware of Truth. If you do choose to become aware of Truth you also become aware that you fear Truth. The experience of Truth is not frightening in Itself. Truth is an experience of wholeness, not lack. So there is no fear in Truth. But when the experience of Truth passes and you think that the self is reality again you find that you are terrified of Truth.

You are pulled back to the experience of the self by your fear of Truth. This is the same as saying you are pulled back to the experience of the self by your attachment to the self. Your fear of Truth *is* your attachment to the self.

Truth is not merely a better personal experience. Truth is formless Being extending infinitely. It is wholly unlike the limited experience of the self. You fear Truth when you identify with a self because Truth seems like a Great Unknown. You are also unconsciously aware that Truth will undo the self. When you identify with a self this feels like Truth would kill *you.*

*Vincent had a direct experience of Truth. It was an experience of boundless joy. It was an experience of wholeness unlike the experience of the self in every way. But afterward he tried to forget about it. He tells himself that it was his imagination or some misfiring of synapses in his brain. He was angry and depressed for a long time afterward. Unconsciously he is terrified by the experience. He thinks it will kill him.*

When you identify with a self your whole experience is the denial of Truth. And the act of denial makes you fear what you deny. Why would you deny something except that it is undesirable? Remember, Truth is in your mind whether or not you are aware of It. When you are not conscious of Truth it is because you deny Truth. So the denial of Truth that is the whole personal experience implies to your mind that Truth is to be feared. And your denial of Truth makes it possible for you to arbitrarily assign any meaning or traits to Truth.

*Lucas claims he will never meditate. He is afraid that if he empties his mind "the Devil" will come into it. The idea of a devil is Lucas' unconscious fear of Truth. To the personal thought system in his mind, with which he is very identified, the Truth is an unknown "evil".*

Add guilt and fear of punishment to your suspicion and fear of the Unknown and death and is it any wonder that the Truth terrifies you? It's a miracle that you have invited Truth into your awareness at all! But of course beyond your unconscious and conscious fear of Truth you know that the Truth is true and that It is benign. This is why you are drawn to It.

Your denial of Truth also makes you unaware that the experience of the self into which you seemed to be born is only a meaningless idea. It has no reality. It is an idea of the impossible given form. Denial blends well with guilt to make it seem that not-Truth is real and a sin for which you will be punished. This seems to justify your suspicions of Truth as frightening unknown and potential killer.

You do not desire the self for anything inherent in the experience of the self. It is a painful, limited experience. But fear of Truth makes the self desirable to you. The self seems to protect you from Truth. The thinking is circular here:

Your identification with a self causes you to fear Truth.

Your fear of Truth causes you to cling to your identification with a self.

You fear Truth *only* in your identification with a self, just as you experience guilt only in your identification with a self. Your identification with a self is your only problem.

11. The self and the body symbolize guilt

Until you unconsciously or consciously choose to know better you identify with a self. You live through the self as though it is you. You protect it and you defend it. You nurture it and you grow it. What happens or does not happen to it determines your moods and how you feel about yourself. In your identification with a self you feel limited and lacking. So you direct the self to fill these needs. You futilely pursue the wholeness, peace, and happiness it can never find for you. And all of this unconsciously fosters guilt in your mind because the self's seeming-reality is the symbol of the death of Truth.

The body represents the self in material form. As not-Truth it is nothing in Truth. But in the story for not-Truth's seeming-reality all forms symbolize the split-mind's triumph over Truth. Form is the "new reality" which replaces Formless Reality. It is the limitation that replaces Limitlessness.

As the opposite of Eternal Truth everything in the universe of form is temporary. Everything eventually "dies". The death of bodies especially represents not-Truth's absolute triumph over Truth. In the new reality Eternal Life is replaced by inevitable death. All of this is only symbolic, of course. In its replacement reality the split-mind only kills off forms of not-Truth. Over and over and over again. Repetition is how it tries to convince itself that it has killed Truth. But Truth continues on untouched by any of it.

The personal thought system is so entranced by death that in some cases it relentlessly drives to suicide an individual who believes strongly in guilt. Suicide is the clearest demonstration of a personal thought system's true intention. It means to kill you. But, again, this can only be symbolic. Killing a body does not kill Truth. The Truth in any mind is untouched by what does or does not happen to a self.

You will notice that guilt strikes you firmly when you are grieving a death. Sometimes this is for a specific reason.

*Irving's father passed away and he feels guilty because the last time they spoke they argued.*

*Nina had always intended to apologize to her sister, Grace, for an estrangement that occurred between them many years before. But now Grace is gone and Nina feels guilty for never making amends.*

Even when you have no story for specific guilt you find yourself haunted by generalized guilt when someone close to you dies. You may even feel guilty hearing about a death of someone not close to you. Every death symbolizes the death of Truth to your unconscious. It reminds you of your guilt for "killing" Truth.

For the personal thought system the body is the symbol of its seeming-reality. So the body is a symbol of guilt. Physical pleasure and pain both focus your attention on the body. They seem to be the "proof" that the body is real. So they reinforce guilt in your mind. But they only make the body real to you if you choose to interpret them that way.

As the opposite of Truth all of not-Truth is inherently limited, imperfect, and disordered. Pain in the body and in the self's life are inevitable. But suffering is a choice. Suffering is caused by the thoughts that you have about the pain. If you have a story for physical pain that it is punishment or that you are a victim then you will turn temporary, passing pain into suffering. You will suffer not just psychologically but the physical pain will be worse, too.

*Whenever Evelyn has one of her grinding headaches she is sure that she is being punished for something. She always finds some mistake she made to which she can associate the headache. When she feels that she deserves the punishment it always seems that the pain is worse.*

*Wayne has a painful congenital condition in his spine. He feels that he is the victim of a cruel god. His victimhood is a large part of identity so he dwells a great deal on his physical pain. Physical pain looms large in his experience.*

Whatever you attend to with your mind grows in your awareness. If you focus on pain then pain grows in your awareness. But if you focus on something else, the pain will fall into the background.

*Craig observed that when he was preoccupied with work he hardly noticed the pain in his broken ankle. He realized that he had the choice to focus on the pain or to let it be and go about his day.*

Your thoughts also affect the body's chemistry and energy, decreasing or increasing its pain.

*Bunny has pain in her spine from a fracture that occurred a few years ago. Over many years she has grown her awareness of Truth. And she has worked out much of the guilt in her mind. She has come to accept that the personal experience will never be perfect. She no longer needs to perfect it because she experiences Perfection in Truth. Without guilt and with acceptance she is more relaxed and feels much less pain than she used to in her spine.*

When you identify with a self you unconsciously and often consciously feel guilty for choosing and experiencing physical pleasure. This is because where pain may seem to come to you unbidden, pleasure is something that you consciously seek to offset the psychological and emotional pain of the personal experience.

What is called *pleasure* are those activities that cause endorphins to be released by the brain. This is what makes the body feel good. That this is something that occurs only in the body is why pleasure does not release guilt. Guilt is an idea in the mind, so physical pleasure only distracts you from guilt. And by seeking to undo psychological and emotional pain through physical pleasure you actually reinforce your belief in the body as your reality. You reinforce guilt in your mind. So "pleasure" is just a label given to a form of pain that is meant to offset other forms of pain.

When you identify with a self you unconsciously and often consciously feel guilty about sex. This is not just because of the pleasure aspect of sex. Reproduction is the split-mind replicating itself to ensure its continuity in its illusion of a new reality. Reproduction validates the self as reality so it reinforces guilt.

Not-Truth's religions do no cause its followers to feel guilty for sex. They only validate the guilt for sex that is already in their minds. In some cases religions do seek to explain the guilt, for example, by linking it to "original sin". And they do seek to mitigate guilt around sex by prescribing which sexual activities are considered appropriate to their god. They must do this because the world is real to them. They need to justify reproduction by believing that it is decreed by their god.

Nothing can undo the link between guilt and sex. Sex is wholly about the self/body so it wholly reinforces the reality of guilt. While you still want to have sex the most you can do is to not interpret it in ways that increase your guilt.

*Alessandro has been growing his awareness of Truth. He used to look to sex as one way of dealing with his pain. But now he turns inward to Truth and resolves his pain at its source in his mind. But he is married and sex is still a way that he and his wife communicate their love to each other. So Alessandro has accepted that with sex come feelings of guilt. He lets guilt come up and he lets it go. He does not judge himself for the sex or for the guilt.*

12. Confusing Love with guilt and sacrifice

To the personal thought system's way of thinking you seem to have "sacrificed" Truth to identify with it. This is the source of guilt in your mind. So sacrifice is the personal thought system's highest value. So much so that to it *to love* means *to sacrifice*. But also *to sacrifice* means *to make guilty*. So *to love* also means *to make guilty*. Love, sacrifice, and guilt are one in the personal thought system.

There is no clearer example of this than in one of not-Truth's religions, Christianity. Its foundation is the story of a god sacrificing his only son to wash away your sins. And the son willingly sacrifices his life for you. Their sacrifices are how they show their love for you. Their love makes you guilty. And if you are one of their followers you in turn must make sacrifices to show your love for them.

*Ramona and Bryan are Christians. When they had children Ramona put her career on hold to raise them and Bryan became the sole source of financial support for the family. Both feel that they have made sacrifices to have the kind of family that they believe their god has ordained. This makes them feel simultaneously superior to and resentful of others who do not make the same choices. Both their superiority and their resentment are intended to make others guilty. They feel that their "love" (guilt toward/sacrifice for) for their god entitles them to greater love (guilt and sacrifice from) from others.*

But you do not have to be religious to believe that love and sacrifice are the same. This belief is just another aspect of the belief that guilt is real. Love = sacrifice = guilt plays out through all of the relationships that the personal thought system forms with others. This is why they are so contentious and full of resentments.

*Ernie feels that when he married he gave up his freedom. He unconsciously feels that he made a sacrifice for love. He expects his wife, Cora, to give up things for the relationship, too. He has asked her to give up her bi-monthly weekend hikes with her friends to spend every weekend with him. But Cora feels that she has made a reasonable compromise by not hiking every weekend. Ernie feels that she is not sacrificing for the relationship so he questions her love for him.*

*Rhonda makes sure her children know how much discomfort she went through when she was pregnant with them, how much their deliveries hurt, and how much she has given up for them over the years. She says she just wants them to know how much she loves them. But really she is trying to make them feel guilty to bind them to her. When they do feel guilty she feels a sense of satisfaction. To her their guilt means they understand and appreciate her. She feels loved. But her children feel attacked and resentful.*

*At work George volunteered to take on a project that no one else wanted. He made this "sacrifice" as a show of love toward his co-workers. He expected gratitude. He feels his co-workers owe him. But his co-workers think that he is just a fool. Now he resents them.*

The belief that love demands sacrifice is another reason that you unconsciously fear Truth. Love is treacherous when you think that It is going to ask you to somehow suffer for It. If you believe that love means sacrifice then you must believe that Total Love would mean total sacrifice.

*Patricia was raised Catholic but gave up the Church after she moved out of her parents' home. She sometimes feels drawn back to religion or spirituality. She has gone to different churches with her friends and she reads popular spiritual books. But in the end she always puts these things aside. Unconsciously she remembers the centrality of sacrifice to Catholic doctrine and she cannot see how this is love. How could a loving Father do that to his Son? She confuses spiritual awareness with religion and does not trust any of it.*

*Adrian's spirituality is based in New Thought teachings but he still feels guilty when he enjoys himself or desires anything in the world. He unconsciously believes that he is supposed to sacrifice for Truth. He does not know that this belief is an obstacle to his growing his awareness of Truth.*

Even if you expect Love to be greater than what you are asked to sacrifice you must feel that you are being punished when you sacrifice. The demand for sacrifice implies your guilt. If you have to pay for or earn Love then you must be unworthy of It.

*Darrell is a Christian minister whose salary is low. He struggles to support his family. He is expected to be on call 24/7 for his congregation. He feels exhausted and grossly underpaid. He feels abandoned by his god but will not consciously acknowledge this. Why would his god abandon him but that he is unworthy? This only makes Darrell sacrifice even more to earn his god's love.*

The personal thought system also teaches you that sacrifice is how to *reduce* guilt. But you would not sacrifice unless you believed that guilt is real. So choosing to sacrifice only reinforces your belief in guilt.

*Steve is chronically broke and emotionally and physically exhausted. He feels driven to give too much to and do too much for others. But he has a sense of satisfaction, too. He feels that he is a "good person". He feels that he is "compassionate". Unconsciously he feels that these sacrifices will reduce his punishment for his guilt. But actually they only reinforce his belief that guilt is real.*

For the personal thought system love is an emotion directed toward others. It is a feeling of attachment, affection, or extreme liking. And because you simply do not know everyone well or like everyone, spiritual counsels to "be your brother's keeper" and to "love your brother as yourself" become twisted into sources for guilt by the personal thought system. You cannot love everyone so you feel guilty.

*Zoe tries hard to love everyone at work but there are just some people that she does not like. She finds them selfish or rude or even mean. She feels that she is failing in her spirituality because she does not love everyone. She does not realize that she is trying to love them with personal love.*

True Love simply is. It is nor personal. It is detached and dispassionate. You can be aware of True Love within you, but you cannot direct It toward anyone. To truly love others means *to come from an awareness of the reality of Love within you.* You do this for your sake not for their sake. You do it to reinforce your awareness of Love.

*Astra doesn't like her brother-in-law, Kenneth. She finds him to be boorish and self-centered and she doesn't like the way that he bullies her sister. But she recognizes that these are just her personal feelings. When the family gets together she doesn't avoid Kenneth but she also does not seek him out. When she must interact with him she comes from her awareness of Love within her just as she does with everyone else. She does this because she wants to remember that she is Love. Personalities are irrelevant for this.*

True Love does not come from a sense of lack in yourself or in others. It comes from an awareness that Wholeness is Reality. Notice that there are two parts to the counsel to "love your brother as yourself". To truly love yourself is to be aware of your Wholeness in Truth. So to truly love another is to be aware of their Wholeness in Truth. This awareness is what you "keep" in mind for them whether or not they are aware of it.

*Gerard's 30 year old brother, Nick, has chosen to not become an adult. Gerard used to run to his brother's rescue emotionally, psychologically, and financially. But as Gerard has grown aware of the Truth within himself he has become aware that the same Truth is in others. He realizes that enabling Nick to remain immature is not the way to love him. He realizes that he was actually disrespecting Nick. Now Gerard is willing to support Nick as Nick supports himself but he refuses to rescue Nick anymore. Nick does not like this. Gerard's boundaries respect him as an adult. They give him an opportunity to grow into adulthood. But it is Nick's choice whether he will grow or find another enabler.*

True Love does not make or demand sacrifice. True Love recognizes that Wholeness *is*. There is no guilt in True Love.

13. Guilt revealed by spiritualizing the self

Remember, you do not have guilt in your mind because there is an absolute-morality decreed by a god that you defied. Your unconscious belief in intrinsic guilt gives rise to an unconscious belief in a god and an absolute-morality.

The self is nothing but a false conception of reality. But guilt makes it seem real to you. Guilt makes it seem subject to an absolute-morality. It grants the self spiritual significance. It *spiritualizes* the self.

Spiritualizing the self confuses Truth and not-Truth. Truth is not a god but the personal thought system experiences It as a Power outside of it. And the personal thought system believes that it is as real as Truth. So spiritualizing the self arises from guilt in your mind and perpetuates guilt in your mind. And it also reinforces your belief in the reality of guilt by conflating the self with Truth.

When you feel that the self "should" or "should not" do something, or you worry about what is right or wrong or good or bad in absolute-moral terms, you spiritualize the self. When you are concerned with the self being right, good, or perfect you are trying to mitigate your guilt toward a god by fixing the self which you think offends that god.

*Quincy belongs to a religion with strict doctrine about behavior and lifestyle. He takes great pride in adhering rigidly to his religion. He openly believes that guilt is real and he feels safe in his god's approval because he lives so well by what he sees as his god's rules. What he does not see is that his righteous behavior does not undo his unconscious guilt. The source of his guilt is not his behavior. The source of his guilt is his belief that the self is real. And his emphasis on behavior only reinforces his belief in the self as his reality, perpetuating his guilt.*

The belief in guilt, a god, and an absolute-morality is in every mind. So whether or not you consciously believe in a power over you, you spiritualize the self.

*Chloe does not consciously believe in a god. But she takes great pride in being what she considers a "good person". She is always concerned with "doing the right thing". If you asked her why she would tell you that she is modeling what is best for society. But her strong feelings that she is "bad" or "wrong" if she is not "good" or "right" indicate that "society" just stands in for her unconscious belief in a power over her that sits in judgment on her.*

*Brandon says he does not believe in a god. He says he does not believe in sin. Brandon is also opposed to his country going to war unless it is directly attacked. When his president takes his country into a war that Brandon thinks is unjustified Brandon argues against the war on social-moral grounds. But the rage and hatred that he feels toward his president indicate that Brandon believes in intrinsic guilt. He sees his president's actions as morally wrong, not just as disruptive to social harmony. Brandon unconsciously believes that there is a power over the world that decrees right and wrong.*

There are certain common questions that arise for many that indirectly and often unconsciously spiritualize the self. They imply or at least hope for a god- or Truth-given meaning for the self and its world. They do not seem to be saying that guilt is real. But they do indirectly state this by not questioning the reality of the self. Though they may sound like genuine, open questions, they are really statements from the personal thought system in the form of questions. What they state is that the self is real. So they state that guilt is real.

For example, "What happens when I die?" implies that the self asking the question exists and that there is some possibility that it is eternal. It is a question that at least hopes to spiritualize the self.

No one aware of Truth would ask this question because they would be aware of the Eternal and know that It is not the time-bound self.

"What is the meaning of life?" and "What is my purpose in life?" both imply that not-Truth has a god- or Truth- given intention. These questions, however, can only be answered by you. And the answers are determined by what you believe is real and true. If you believe that not-Truth is true then your answer is that life's meaning and your purpose are to negate Truth. So guilt is life's meaning and your purpose. The personal thought system will not say this directly, of course. But it will give the world meaning and the self a purpose. Whether seeming to be given by a god or by the self in the hopes of pleasing a god they would validate the reality of not-Truth.

*Jeff has a personality that is given to teaching. He feels that his god wants him to teach others about God to change them and the world to be in line with God. So he writes spiritual books and goes on speaking tours. Over time he wonders why he is not experiencing the liberation and peace that he expected doing "God's work". What he does not see is that his belief that the self is real is his belief that guilt is real. And this is his obstacle to peace.*

*Shawna doesn't know if she believes in a god or not. But she has decided that the meaning of life is love. She figures that if there is a god then this view of life will please him. Her purpose in life, then, is to love others. She has become a nurse to express this. She starts her career enthusiastically but in time she just finds herself emotionally drained. Because the world is real to her she has been trying to love others from the unconscious belief that guilt is real. So in her work she has been reinforcing lack instead of coming from an awareness of Wholeness. And this has drained her.*

When you know that Truth is Reality you know that the world and the self have no meaning or purpose in themselves. *You* give them temporary purpose *for you* by using them to grow your awareness of Truth. You recognize that this is your choice, not something given by a power over you.

*Each morning when she awakens Gita reminds herself that only the Truth is True. She makes remembering Truth the purpose of her day. This gives everything the same meaning and purpose, simplifying her life. She communes with Truth in the morning. Then throughout the day she brings her mind back to Truth whenever she has a moment to do so. She stays present and mindful. If something disturbs her peace she uses it to remind her to turn her mind inward to Truth again. She does this not because it is right or good in the eyes of some distant god. She does this because she wants to be at peace now.*

Another common question, "Why do bad things happen to good people?" implies that there is, or at least should be, an absolute-morality that guides the world. It gives the world spiritual significance. Of course, the designation of what is "good" or "bad" is arbitrarily determined by any personal thought system's values of the moment.

*Brian broke his leg playing football in college in the early sixties. It didn't heal properly and he was left with a limp. At the time he thought this was a bad thing because it ended his football career. But when the Vietnam War escalated and his friends were drafted into a war they did not understand and did not support he realized that his imperfect leg was a blessing. It kept him out of the war.*

*When Bella lost her son in an accident Jillian thought it was a tragedy. She had always liked Bella. To Jillian a bad thing had happened to a good person. But years later Jillian felt betrayed by an action of Bella's and she thought that maybe Bella was actually evil and that's why earlier God had taken her son.*

What happens in form is the result of cause and effect at the level of form. But it has no meaning. Any meaning that you see in the world you put there to see.

<u>14. Cherished beliefs that spiritualize the self</u>

Not-Truth's religions openly spiritualize not-Truth. They teach that a god made and controls what happens in the universe of form. This god determines absolute-morality. The self affects this god by pleasing or displeasing him. Religions' underlying belief is that both a spirit within you and a body and a world that seem to surround it are real. But, again, religions only give outward shape to a universal unconscious belief in guilt. They are simply honest about their belief in guilt. They reinforce guilt because they believe intrinsic guilt is reality.

There are many cherished religious, metaphysical, and spiritual beliefs that spiritualize the personal experience. They come from your belief in guilt and they reinforce your belief in guilt. You must look at these and be willing to release them if you want to be free of guilt. Some of them are examined here:

You may believe that you will receive peace only by a god's "grace". This means that you believe that your god could choose to arbitrarily grant you peace despite your guilt and imperfection. You believe that the self and guilt are real.

*Gloria has been on a spiritual path for a long time but she has yet to experience real peace. Instead of looking for her obstacles to peace she works at being good and righteous in her attitudes, thoughts, and actions, hoping to receive peace through God's grace.*

*Justin has no expectation of experiencing inner peace. He knows that he is a sinner and that if peace comes to him it will only be through the unmerited grace of his god.*

If you pray to a god in the hopes that he will grant what you want in the world you state that you believe that guilt is real.

*Jorge's son, Ernesto, was hit in the head by a ball while playing baseball. Ernesto was knocked unconscious. Jorge prayed to his god for Ernesto's safe recovery. His underlying belief is that the world and his god are both real. He believes that his god makes things happen in the world. So he petitions his god to make things happen the way he wants. Jorge also wonders if he and his son are being punished for their guilt through this incident.*

When you feel that you experience Truth or a god in the world you are only projecting them into the world. You confuse an internal experience with an external cause. You confuse Truth and not-Truth, giving reality to guilt and maintaining it in your mind.

*Luke feels God in nature. Camping is for him what a church, temple, or mosque is for others. At an early age, while he was walking in the woods, he allowed his mind to quiet and Truth came into his awareness as a palpable Presence within him. Since then he opens himself to Truth whenever he is in nature. So in his mind the source of his internal experience of Peace is nature. He lives a dual life of conflict in the city and peace in nature. Both are real to him. But if he wanted he could experience Truth at any time anywhere by simply turning his mind inward and being willing to experience It.*

Beliefs in an individual soul or spirit, pre-ordination, and/or reincarnation are beliefs that individuality is real and eternal. So they are beliefs that guilt is real and eternal, too.

*Neela believes that she has an individual spirit. She believes that she chose the life that she is living before she was born into it. She also believes that if she does not become enlightened in this lifetime she will continue to be reborn until she does reach enlightenment. She has spent so much time in this lifetime trying to reach enlightenment that she cannot understand why she does not have more peace. What she does not see is that these beliefs imply that the self is real, so guilt is real. In fact, she unconsciously feels guilty for making this life. And she unconsciously feels that being reincarnated would be a punishment for not attaining enlightenment this time around. These unconscious beliefs frighten her and block her awareness of the whole and perfect Truth within her right now.*

The belief that you must earn, attain, or achieve God, Truth, enlightenment, etc. reveals that you believe that the self is real and that it is you. You feel that the way to undo guilt is to change the self to make it more Truth-like. But the self has nothing to do with the Truth in you. The Truth in you is whole and perfect and untouched by the self. Trying to change the self to make it more Truth-like is actually the way to hold onto the self and guilt.

*Estelle has been working on her mind for decades trying to attain enlightenment. She experiences some periods of intense doubt that confuse her. She is baffled by how judgmental she still is. She does not see that she has been trying to convince the personal thought system of Truth. It is the personal thought system that doubts, not her. And she has been trying to "enlighten" the personal thought system by trying to make it non-judgmental, or more Truth-like. But it will not change. She is spiritualizing the self and holding onto guilt by trying to change it. She has not yet accepted that Truth is already whole and complete within her. She only has to release the self to see this.*

You may feel a desire to directly spiritualize the self by applying your awareness of Truth to the self's life.

*Byron has experienced Truth. He wants to extend his awareness of Truth into his life in the world. He has decided to develop a universal ethic based on the concepts of universal love and oneness. But he notices that as he gets to work on this he loses his peace. He does not see that he is making the same mistake that transforms true spiritual awareness into a religion. He is spiritualizing the self because he thinks that both the self and his spiritual experiences are real. This belief is his obstacle to staying aware of Truth.*

*When she embarked on a spiritual path Molly stopped watching violent TV shows and movies. She did not do this because of an authentic change in values. She did this because she felt that violence is out of accord with Truth. She felt that she "should not" watch violence because she unconsciously believes that doing so displeases a god. She is trying to change the self to be more Truth-like, reinforcing her guilt.*

*Rip is on a path of spiritual awakening. He lives in poverty because he believes that money and material wealth are bad. He does not see that he is confusing Truth and not-Truth by projecting absolute-moral meaning onto meaningless forms. He does not see that he believes that guilt is real and that this is his obstacle to peace.*

The belief that unseen forces, like energy or "supernatural" or unexplained phenomena, are or come from a god or Truth is the belief that some forms of not-Truth are true. And if any of not-Truth is true guilt is true.

*Becca listens to physicists discuss unseen particles and energy that make up matter. Because energy cannot be seen with the eyes she thinks it is the same as Formlessness. She thinks that Truth takes the form of energy. This belief spiritualizes form for her, reinforcing her belief in form's reality. And this perpetuates guilt in her mind. This confusion of not-Truth and Truth will be an obstacle for her as she tries to advance in her awareness of Truth.*

*For Akele anything non-material, like energy, ghosts, psychic readings, etc. is "spiritual". She believes they are the same as or come from Truth. This confusion makes it impossible for her to sort out Truth and not-Truth. And this keeps her in guilt.*

Truth is Formless Being. Form, seen or unseen, is the opposite of Truth. Truth never takes or makes form.

Another way that the belief that Truth takes form shows up is in the belief that synchronicity comes from Truth.

*Luigi has noticed that as he meditates and becomes more mindful he sees patterns in events. He feels that this is Truth working in his life. But it is really just his greater awareness of what is going on around him. His belief that Truth and not-Truth can blend only maintains guilt in his mind. It is an obstacle to his awareness of Truth.*

Your identification with form (self/body) is the source of guilt in your mind. So when you want to use your mind to heal the body you do so because you identify with the body. This reinforces guilt in your mind. And then when you fail to heal the body with your mind you feel that you are failing. You feel guiltier.

*Deirdre has arthritis. She has read metaphysical books that teach that disorders in the body are caused by unconscious guilt. She has spent many years trying to dig out the guilt in her mind. She has found and released much guilt, but her arthritis has not changed. She keeps digging for more guilt, which the personal thought system is happy to supply. She does not see that she is making guilt real to herself by identifying with the body. And she is also making guilt real to herself by continuing to look for guilt. She unconsciously feels that there must be something wrong with her for failing to heal. She feels guiltier for not healing.*

You cannot want to change form and also release your mind from your belief in it. Your wanting to change form means it is real to you and you value it. So the desire to use your mind to manifest a better personal life shows that you believe that the self is you and that you are guilty.

*Gemma has been learning how to attract and manifest what she wants in the self's life. She's been using her mind to change the self's relationship to the world of form. Her desire to do this reveals her belief that she is the self and that the world of form is her source. These are real to her, so guilt is real to her. She may master attraction but she will not have peace until she releases the self as her identity.*

When you spiritualize not-Truth you see a hierarchy within not-Truth. Those things that the personal thought system judges as right and good you see as true and those that it judges as wrong or bad you see as not true. For example, a whole, healthy body or a life for the self where it has all that it wants you see as more Truth-like.

Some forms of spiritualizing not-Truth are temporarily useful. For example, you may find "Teacher of Truth" too abstract an idea to trust It. If this is the case then the Teacher of Truth may be embodied for you as an historical spiritual figure, like Jesus, or as an "enlightened being" with you now. But in the long run these will fall away as you become aware of the Truth within you.

*When he began on a spiritual path Pascal felt the presence of Jesus in his life. For many years this was the image he had of the Teacher of Truth. But as he became more aware of the Truth within himself he found that holding onto the image of a person as a symbol for Truth was an obstacle to peace for him. It kept him self-identified and it made Truth seem outside of him. Pascal gradually let go of the image of Jesus and allowed himself to simply experience the still quiet of Truth within.*

You may have beliefs that attempt to alleviate guilt by seeing not-Truth as a manifestation of a spiritual being. For example, you may believe that the universe of form is a spiritual being learning something, often about itself. This is an attempt to intellectually deny guilt by stating that the personal experience has a positive intention. But the need to learn implies a lack. So the being in need of the learning experience would be imperfect. Beliefs like these not only spiritualize the self they spiritualize guilt!

Another form of spiritualizing the self and guilt is the belief that a god made the world because it was lonely or bored. Loneliness and boredom are forms of lack. They are not aspects of Wholeness. These beliefs make guilt true not just for the self but for its god as well.

You spiritualize the self when you first become aware of Truth because the personal experience is so real to you. You expect that you are meant to change it to be more Truth-like rather than to let it go. This early stage is impossible to avoid, especially since it is heavily reinforced by the personal thought system. The personal thought system initially resists you looking inward. But it soon realizes that it can use spiritual ideas to validate itself and increase your guilt and fear of looking inward. It does not care if you want to make the self more "spiritual" as long as you continue to believe in it. But if you do not move on from this stage you will continue in guilt and fear.

*Audrey did not consider herself either spiritual or religious. But while going through a personal crisis she had a profound dream one night where she experienced Limitlessness and a deep sense of knowing with absolute certainty that everything was okay. Afterward she spoke with a friend about it. Her friend suggested that Audrey look into Buddhism to get in touch with What she experienced in the dream. But Audrey finds the meditation practice too uncomfortable. She had one moment of unconscious willingness to experience Truth but the unconscious guilt in her mind prevents her from opening to Truth again. However, she knows that What she experienced is real and she can't forget about It. So instead she attends a popular*

*Christian mega-church that spiritualizes the self with its teachings of absolute-moral meaning. She unconsciously finds that the church mirrors her experiences of Truth and guilt, both of which are real to her. She finds it more comfortable to embrace, rather than face, her belief that guilt is real.*

*Stan has been on a New Thought spiritual path for a long time. He has a self-image as a "spiritual person". He works hard at having what he sees as correct "spiritual" thoughts, attitudes, and behaviors. But he wonders why he does not have inner peace. He does not realize that inner peace is the result of being aware of Truth, not of being a spiritual person. He does not see that he still believes the self is real, so he still believes that guilt is real. And this is his obstacle to peace.*

It may seem odd to say that you will experience grief as you release guilt. But you are likely to have some feeling of loss as cherished beliefs that spiritualize the self fall away. This will pass, however, as you experience the relief of being released from guilt. You will realize that your attachment to these beliefs was attachment to guilt.

*Jordan loved the image of himself as a "child of God". He enjoyed the role of striving-to-be-good-enough "son" to a loving-but-judgmental higher-being "Father". It gave context and purpose to his life to be a "good person" who always tried to "do right". But he has come to be aware of the Truth within. This experience conflicts with his concept of a power over and outside of him. He feels sad to learn that there is no such thing as a father-god. He feels sad to release the "child of God" image of himself. But he also feels relief. He realizes that he was driven by guilt. The sadness passes but the sense of freedom remains.*

*It makes Adawina sad to realize that her loved ones who passed away did not "go on". She will never see them again. But she feels whole when she is centered in Truth. So she realizes that when she is sad she is identifying with a limited self. And when she does that she looks to others to feel whole. But there is no lack in Truth. She does not need "loved ones" in Truth to make her feel whole. She has the choice to identify with a limited, lacking self who is always seeking for wholeness. Or she can attend to the Truth in her mind and feel whole now.*

15. The manifest effect of your awareness of Truth

As you advance in your awareness of Truth it does have a positive effect on the self's life in the world. You may be tempted to interpret this effect as spiritualizing the self. But spiritualizing the self is something that you do because of guilt and to attempt to alleviate guilt. And the manifest effect of your awareness of Truth on the self's life happens naturally and effortlessly. It does not happen for a purpose. It is ultimately meaningless.

Formless Truth is what your mind is. And the personal experience is one of form, or not-Truth. Your story for the self is in your mind. So both Truth and the personal story are in your mind, but they never intersect. The personal story is never a part of Truth. It never affects Truth. And Truth never takes form. But *your awareness* of Truth corrects your mind back to its natural state of wholeness. And this manifests in the self's unfolding story. The self's attitudes, behavior, choices, and energy change for the better when you are aware of Truth. This changes the self's relationship to the world and the world's response to it. This can make it seem like there is a relationship between Truth and the self and its world. But really it is just that both Truth and the self are related to you. Truth is your Cause and the self is your mind's effect at the level of form.

*As Natalie has worked out the guilt in her mind her unconscious belief in her unworthiness has dropped away. This has changed her relationship to the world through her attitudes and behavior but also at the energetic level. She finds opportunities presenting themselves to her in her career and personal life that would not have presented before because her belief in her unworthiness would have blocked them.*

*Elliot had very low self-esteem. He was attracted to women whom he allowed to use him. He couldn't say no to his boss or his staff at work. He was emotionally drained by others' drama because he felt his worth came from fixing others' problems. But he allowed Truth into his awareness and he found himself guided to self-help books that made him realize that his problems came from his poor self-image. In time, as the Truth became true for him, he found himself building healthy boundaries with others. Unhealthy relationships fell away. He only has healthy, respectful relationships in his life now. Truth did not go out into the self's life and change it. But his awareness of Truth changed his mind and this changed the self's life.*

*Avery was diagnosed with multiple sclerosis many years ago. He took the prescribed medication and did a minimum of self-care. But as his awareness of Truth has grown he has realized that he does not have to suffer. He asks the Teacher of Truth to guide him as he cares for the body. Avery has found a supportive community online and has greatly improved his self-care. This has done much to improve his quality of life.*

*As the Truth has become true for Molly the energy in the self's body has changed. Latent illnesses which would have struck her in middle age have been put off.*

When the self's life improves because of your awareness of Truth you may be tempted to use your awareness of Truth to manipulate the self's life in ways that you think you need to for peace and happiness. But this means you still believe the source of your happiness is the self and its life in the world. This is the same old confusion of cause and effect.

Your awareness of Truth is the cause of your peace and happiness. And the self is a meaningless effect of your mind. So the self, its body, and its world do not cause your sense of peace or conflict. If you want to manipulate them then you must believe that they are your reality and the cause of your peace or conflict. And it is this belief that is the source of your sense of guilt. So as soon as you decide to use your awareness of Truth to serve the self you remove yourself from the awareness that you already have peace and happiness in Truth.

*Beverly noticed that her life improved when Truth came into her awareness. She had some peace and her relationship to the world was more harmonious. She was still very identified with the self, however, so she felt that changing the self's life for the better was the purpose of being aware of Truth. This shifted her attention away from Truth to the self. So she was back in lack again and she lost her peace.*

To order cause and effect correctly, first you become aware of Truth. Then this awareness will manifest in the self's life as a natural effect.

*Claudio's life was a mess. His relationships were rocky, he was deeply in debt, and he was in a job he hated. He hit bottom and unconsciously called for help. The Teacher of Truth in his mind answered in his subconscious. Claudio found himself drawn to self-help and spiritual books. He eventually entered therapy and invited Truth into his conscious awareness. All of these helped him to feel better about himself. He came to feel worthy of a healthy, peaceful life. Over time he dealt with his emotional issues and learned how to relate better with others. He simplified his life, cleaned up his finances, and found a job that he enjoys.*

## Seeing Guilt in the world

16. Personal perspective and projection

Truth is One, or the same throughout Itself. In Truth there is only Truth. For the Mind of Truth this translates into the Law of Mind that *Mind only knows Itself.*

Even in its split state mind is under this law. This means that when you think with the personal thought system you see the world of form through the filter of your personal story. This makes your *personal perspective.*

*Ben and Jan are canoodling on a park bench on a warm spring day.*

*Kyle, an 8 year old boy whose hormones have not yet kicked in, thinks that they are gross. He makes sure to go around them in a wide circle.*
*Alice, who was taught that emotions are private and not to be shared, thinks public displays of affection are inappropriate. She huffs and puffs in disapproval as she passes them.*
*Chuck thinks a man who is affectionate with his woman in public is weak. He feels contempt for Ben and sneers at him.*
*Keetcha is a young woman who wants to be in love and thinks that they are beautiful and lucky.*
*Diane has fond memories of early courtship with her husband and thinks that they are cute.*
*Paul recently lost his husband and seeing the loving young couple triggers a wave of grief in him.*
*Tally, who attracts and is attracted to abusive men, thinks Jan is a fool and is setting herself up to be hurt.*

Everyone seems to share a world of form. But everyone actually lives in their personal perspective. And they feel that others are wrong when they do not share their perspective.

*Arturo has been a petty thief for most of his life. He began as a young child by stealing small items from family members as a way to feel empowered. As he grew he occasionally shop-lifted and stole from friends and teachers. As an adult he steals small things off of co-workers' desks and office supplies from his work-place.*

*Arturo's world-view is that everyone is a thief of some sort. He interprets others' motives from this perspective, whether they be acquaintances, family, strangers, or governments. For him, this is simply fact. He does not see that he perceives others from his own life experience. When others do not share his world-view he thinks that they are blind fools.*

*Bao was left by her mother with an indifferent father when she was very small. She felt abandoned. She doesn't let anyone get close to her because she expects that they will abandon her. And she feels that it is easier to be alone than to be with someone and then to lose them.*

*She does have relatives, casual acquaintances, and co-workers. When anyone leaves her life for whatever reason she takes it personally and feels abandoned. She will not be reassured that their leaving is not about her. She does not see that she is interpreting other people's actions through her own expectation of abandonment. To her it is a fact that no one really loves her and that all will eventually leave her. To her the world is a place of abandonment.*

Another way to say that the Mind of Truth knows only Itself is to say that It extends Itself everywhere, always. In your mind's split state your mind extends only when it is aware of Truth. This means that when you are aware of Truth, Truth is what you experience despite what appears in the universe of form. Truth is What you know to be True.

*Gordon is a physician. He has spent many years growing his awareness of Truth. He spends his days with people who come to him with all sorts of physical and psychological complaints. But he brings his mind back to Truth throughout each day and reminds himself that only the Truth is true. He sees that his patients do not know this. He sees that they believe very much in their stories and their worlds. But he also knows that their misbeliefs are not true. Only the Truth in their minds is true. No matter what shows up, Gordon rests in peace throughout each day.*

Since the personal thought system is not-Truth, or the denial of Truth, it distorts the Law of Mind into *projection*. Projection is *extension + denial*. When you think with the personal thought system you see your own mind but you deny that it is your own mind that you see. So your personal perspective is a projection from your personal story, but you deny that it comes from you. You think that what you see is reality.

Since the personal thought system is a thought system of guilt, guilt taints your projections from it. The guilt that you see seems to be outside of you and real. Looking back at the example above, Arturo's personal perspective is a projection of a world of thieves. This guilty world does not seem to him like a collection of beliefs and ideas in his own mind. It seems like a real world around him. He may acknowledge his own guilt, but he justifies it as his defense against a world that is guiltier.

Because projection employs denial when you project away beliefs, thoughts, and ideas they seem to be outside of you. They seem to make a reality in which you passively find yourself.

17. Projection and victimhood

Sometimes projections of guilt are related to specific violations of social-morality. Sometimes you consciously feel guilty for a violation but you do not see how your guilt informs your interpretation of others.

*Linda is in Gail's circle of close friends. For several months Gail has been having an affair with Linda's husband. She is conscious of feeling very guilty. Whenever someone in their circle of friends says anything critical of Linda, Gail attacks them. In her guilt over her affair with Linda's husband she unconsciously sees others as disproportionately guilty when they say something negative about Linda. She unconsciously tries to mitigate her guilt over hurting Linda by protecting Linda from what she sees as further attacks.*

At other times you see your guilt for a specific social violation only in others.

*Burt belongs to a religion that has a strict prohibition against homosexual behavior. When he was 12-years old Burt experimented sexually with another boy. He felt so much shame and terror, however, that he soon broke off the friendship and repressed his memories of it.*

*Burt is now an adult and is clearly heterosexual in orientation and behavior. But he is unconsciously guilty about that one episode of experimentation as a child. And he is also unconsciously afraid that it means that he is gay. He hates openly gay people because they unconsciously remind him of his own guilt and his fear that he is like them. He wishes that they would go away. He has spent his adult life working to restrict the rights of gay people because he hopes that it will drive them back into the closet. And he unconsciously hopes that preventing gay people from having equal rights with heterosexuals will serve as amends to his disapproving god for his own sin against him.*

The personal thought system's projections of guilt do not come only from specific incidences in the personal self's story. Guilt is the lens through which you look out at the world when you think with the personal thought system. Projecting it away is supposed to be the way to get rid of it in your own mind. But you only believe in guilt in the world when you believe in guilt in you. So projecting guilt away will not get rid of it. It will actually preserve guilt in your mind because you cannot release it if you believe that it is outside of you.

*Brad has been reading about how guilt is not real. He uses this idea to repress any feelings of guilt that he would feel for his own thoughts, attitudes, or behavior. But he continues to openly judge others. He does not see that this reveals that he still believes in his own guilt. It is the same to believe in guilt in others as to believe in guilt in himself.*

The personal thought system cannot make you completely unaware of the guilt within you. So sometimes you do feel guilty. But projection ensures that you are not aware that *all* of the guilt that you see comes from your belief in the guilt in you. It allows you to feel that you may *sometimes* be guilty but the world is *always* guilty. If you are not innocent you are at least less guilty than others.

*Kalinda is self-employed. She has chosen to not pay taxes. She deals with her guilt for not doing her part by feeling that she is "not as bad as" the very wealthy. What she owes is very small compared to them. They make millions but get tax breaks and find loopholes to avoid paying their full share of taxes.*

When you project ideas outside of you onto a meaningless world of form they do not seem like only ideas. They seem like reality. So when you identify with a self you believe that you are a powerless victim of a guilty world. And your personal story is the filter that gives particular shape to your guilt.

*Brandy has low self-esteem. She unconsciously feels unworthy of love or respect from others. She unconsciously attracts and is attracted to people who treat her poorly because this is what she feels she deserves. But in her mind she is a victim of the people who treat her poorly. She tries to be a nice person. But others are so mean and she cannot understand why. She is innocent and they are guilty. She sees a guilty world of mean people through the filter of her personal story of unworthiness.*

*Kent's parents were drug addicts and his childhood was spent shuttling between foster homes and his parents' home. For him the world is a cold place where you have to make it on your own or not make it at all. He is very driven and outwardly successful. But he doesn't trust anyone. He pushes people away then blames them for abandoning him. He sees a guilty world of people he cannot trust through the filter of his personal story of abandonment.*

*Gil is a young African-American man who grew up in the projects of a major U.S. city. He has heard all of his life about the historical and institutional racism that keeps black men down. He has sometimes witnessed it himself. But he has adopted an identity of black-victim-of-a-white-racist-world and often the racism that he sees comes only from his interpretation of events. He sees a guilty racist world through the filter of his personal story of belonging to an historically oppressed group.*

In your identification with a self you are not in your natural state. So you are in pain, conflicted, and you feel incomplete. When you project guilt onto others you give your power to them. You unconsciously see them as the source of your feelings of lack and pain. You not only blame them for your feelings of discomfort but you feel that they should fix you and make you whole. Anytime you are unhappy with another it is because they have failed to play a role that you assigned to them. You unconsciously set them up to be guilty so that you can be their innocent victim.

*Amelia has a lot of insecurities and anxieties. Gavin is successful, strong, and capable. She expected that when she married Gavin she would feel secure. But her insecurities and anxieties are still there. She unconsciously blames Gavin for failing to fix her. She often makes verbal digs at him, which push him away. She then blames him for emotionally abandoning her.*

*Mara's sister and her family have come to live with Dan and Mara's family for a couple of months while their house is being built. They have different values and habits and Dan finds them all annoying in so many little ways. He sets boundaries but he finds that he constantly has to enforce them. He unconsciously expects them to be grateful toward him. He expects them to understand and respect his boundaries. In his mind they are not meeting these expectations. So he feels he is their victim.*

Victimhood is the default setting for all personal thought systems. You can observe this in yourself and in others. Notice how often during one day you feel hurt, defensive, or angry with others. Listen to how often others' conversations are about how they are put upon by others. People take great pleasure and pride in being victims when they identify with a self. Remember, guilt validates and protects the personal thought system. It does not matter whether you see guilt in yourself or in others. It is just important to it that you believe that guilt is real.

You might be tempted right now to defensively (guiltily) argue that the world is a harsh place. The personal experience *is* the opposite of Truth. It is one of limitation, lack, and loss. And the world is made up of guilty-feeling, frightened people trying to deal with guilt, fear, limitation, lack, and loss in ineffective and dysfunctional ways. So pain is an inevitable part of the personal experience. But you can just accept this and deal with facts and not project meaning. Perceiving yourself as a victim is a choice, not a fact.

*Delward's boss, Robert, refuses to take responsibility for anything. When he makes mistakes he always blames someone who works under him. Because Delward's position is right under Robert's, Robert more often than not makes Delward look responsible for his own mistakes. This puts Delward's career at risk.*

*Delward has been growing his awareness of Truth for many years. He does not expect people to be perfect. He knows that only the Truth within is perfect. He understands projection and has worked through much of the guilt in his mind. If Delward wanted to listen to the personal thought system in his mind he would have a whole story for how Robert is guilty and how he is Robert's victim. But he has worked out enough guilt in his own mind to see that Robert's dysfunction has no meaning in itself. It is not wrong or bad. It is just part of an imperfect world.*

*Delward also knows that he cannot change Robert. For Robert to overcome his guilt and fear, take responsibility for his life, and stop making life hard for those around him, Robert is going to have to want to change.*

*So Delward has two choices: stay in this job as is or leave. He values himself too much to stay in a job with these kinds of frustrations. He decides to leave to find a job working with relatively healthier people.*

*Belinda's son was one of three murdered by a mentally ill man who went on a killing spree. If she wanted to listen to the personal thought system in her mind she would see herself as a victim of the man who killed her son, the gun manufacturer, the family of the mentally ill shooter who did not get him help, and the system that let him out of prison for an earlier crime. But she has grown her awareness of Truth and worked out much of the guilt in her own mind. She grieves for her son, but she does not see guilt. She knows that the shooter was mentally ill. And she accepts that the world is filled with imperfect people who make mistakes. She knows that none of this is real. It is all a passing idea of tragedy, not a real tragedy. Only the Truth is true.*

As you learn about the personal thought system and how it interprets the world to make you feel that you are a victim you may begin to feel that you are a victim of *it*. This is occurring when you find yourself afraid of, hating, or attacking the personal thought system. This is just another manifestation of your belief in your own guilt. You fear, hate, and attack the personal thought system when you project responsibility for your choices through it onto it. This is further abdication of your power to it to avoid the guilt that you believe is real. Remember, the personal thought system has no power over you. Its power comes from you. It is only a mistaken collection of ideas about reality. What you do through the personal thought system has no effect on Truth. You have no reason for guilt.

Although the personal thought system can seem to attack you and to harm you it is really benign because it is not real. Any harm that you feel comes to you from it means that you still identify as a self. The personal thought system can seem to harm what it makes of you (self), but it never touches the Truth in you.

When you feel like a victim of *anything* you are identifying with a self. As a self you feel powerless over others, nature, the personal thought system, and a god that is supposed to have power over you. You give your power away to these ideas. But in Truth you are invulnerable. The Power within you is the Power that is.

18. Absolute-moral meaning as reality

Specifically, what you project from the personal thought system that makes the world of form seem so real to you is *absolute-moral meaning* (right/wrong, good/bad). Projections of absolute-moral meaning *apply* the belief that guilt is real. And guilt comes from the belief that the world of form is real. If this seems circular, it is:

Unconscious denial of Truth causes an experience of a world of form as reality.

Belief in a world of form as reality causes unconscious guilt.

Unconscious guilt causes projections of absolute-moral meaning onto the world of form.

Projections of absolute-moral meaning validate your belief in a world of form as reality.

Belief in a world of form as reality reinforces your unconscious denial of Truth.

This circularity is maintained by the denial aspect of projection. To say that you are unconscious of something in your mind is to say that you deny it. This is why the only way to release the personal thought system and be at peace is to bring to conscious awareness what the personal thought system denies. And these are Truth and your belief in guilt.

Your personal perspective is the inevitable filter through which you look out at the world because the mind always sees itself. Projections from it are tainted with guilt because they are perpetuations of your belief in your personal story as your reality. But these are simply an ongoing context for your experience in the world.

Overt projections of guilt show up as judgments of "wrong" or "bad" with regard to the self or its world. They show up in feelings of "should" and "shouldn't". Look back at the examples of projection onto the couple necking on the park bench offered in part 16. All of the observers see through the filter of their personal story. They unconsciously see guilt because their belief in their personal stories is the source of guilt in their minds. This is all that occurs for Keetcha, Diane, and Paul. But Kyle, Alice, and Chuck see something wrong with the couple. They project guilty meaning onto what they see. And Tally sees nothing wrong with the couple as they are at that moment but she projects into the future a story of inevitable guilt on Ben's part.

Overt projections of guilt give absolute-moral meaning to what you see. And absolute-moral meaning seems to give the universe of form substance and reality by spiritualizing it. (For many examples of this see parts 13 and 14). But withdraw your projections of absolute-moral meaning and you see that the universe of form is a blank canvas. It has no meaning in itself.

*Mindy was listening to a friend recount the story of a plane crash that she'd seen on television. Mindy was feeling upset and realized that she was projecting moral meaning onto the story. She was thinking of the plane crash as wrong rather than as simply a tragic fact of life in the world. She reminded herself that only the Truth is true. This allowed her to release her judgment of absolute-moral meaning on the plane crash. The emotional charge that she felt fell away and she rested in peace.*

*Tang used to feel that the world was a frightening, dangerous place. He felt under constant attack by others. But he has grown his awareness of Truth and he has released much guilt from his own mind. Through the self he still experiences lack, loss, and disorder. But it all passes and he lets it go without judgment. He sees that the world is full of others in pain who still think that their pain is real. But he merely observes this without projecting meaning onto it. Without his projections of moral meaning onto the world of form it is meaningless and benign to him. He finds fulfillment and meaning in his awareness of the Truth within.*

As long as the world seems to have absolute-moral meaning for you it will seem compellingly real to you. But its absolute-moral meaning comes only from your own projected thoughts. If you want to spin out of the cycle of *belief in not-Truth, guilt, projections of moral meaning, belief in not-Truth* you have to be willing to look at how you make the world real to yourself through your belief in intrinsic guilt. And when you have completely released guilt from your mind you will accept that *only* the Truth is true. You will have complete peace.

<u>19. Judging or merely observing</u>

When you project absolute-moral meaning, or judge, you are thinking with the personal thought system in your mind. It responds immediately and emotionally to any situation. Any emotional charge about a situation or your or another's attitudes, behavior, appearance, or words indicates that you see absolute-moral meaning. You believe in intrinsic guilt.

*Ben is grossly obese. When he walked into the waiting room Becky felt immediate disgust. She does not feel his size is a meaningless fact. She feels that it is wrong.*

It may seem obvious that a judgment of *wrong* or *bad* is a projection of guilt. But a judgment of *right* or *good* is also a projection of guilt. It implies that guilt is real, if not in this particular person or situation. Any judgment gives meaning to forms without meaning. And when the world has meaning for you it seems real to you and this reinforces guilt in your mind.

*Ellen did not notice Ben's size so much as his clothes. He is a well-dressed man and she feels great approval of this. Her strong feelings indicate that she judges against those who do not dress to her standards. While she does not see Ben as guilty she still believes that guilt is real.*

If you feel no emotional charge then no judgment is occurring. You are not thinking with the personal thought system. You are merely observing.

*Gaston also saw Ben walk into the waiting room. He couldn't help but observe that Ben is obese but he feels nothing about it and turns back to his magazine.*

While the personal thought system's responses are immediate you do not have to hold onto them. You can release them in the recognition that they give meaning to the meaningless.

*Becky felt and heard the personal thought system in her mind judge against Ben. But then she turned her mind inward and remembered that only the Truth is true. This released her from needing to give meaning to an appearance without any meaning in itself. She feels relief as guilt lifts from her mind. No longer blocked by her judgment on Ben and feeling filled with Love she smiles at him.*

You judge yourself "right" and others "wrong" in an unconscious attempt to convince yourself that you are not guilty. But generalized feelings of guilt will make you judge against yourself. In an effort to explain the guilt that you feel the personal thought system turns facts about the self into something "wrong".

*Adam is motivated by creativity rather than by money. This is just an aspect of his personality. But he feels that a "real man" is one who is financially well-off. He feels guilty for not making a lot of money. His judgment turns a neutral personality trait into something "wrong" to hold against himself.*

The personal experience is one of loss, lack, and limitation. But judgment turns inevitable pain into suffering.

*Charlene lost her best, friend, Lance, in a terrorist attack. But her judgment that his death was wrong turns her grief into suffering. She takes the attacks personally and sees herself as a victim. She is angry and depressed. She feels that her life is out of her control.*

As you learn about guilt, projection, and judgment you will respond strongly to others when you think that they project and judge. This is because the guilt that their judging reveals is in their mind mirrors the guilt in your mind.

*As Bill grows his awareness of Truth and learns about how the personal thought system functions he finds it harder to be around others. Their constant judging irritates him. He judges against their judging because the guilt in their minds reflects the guilt in his own mind. Guilt is still very real to him.*

Sometimes you may think that others are judging when you are judging. If you want to release guilt you have to pay attention to your own emotional charges.

*Kelly was speaking with her friend, Lee Anne, about an ex-boyfriend. Though he never hurt Kelly, when he was angry he would yell in her face, shake his fists, pound on walls and tables, and throw things. She said she broke up with him because he was "aggressive". Lee Anne pointed out that by using that word Kelly was being judgmental. But for Kelly "aggressive" was simply a descriptive word. She felt no emotional charge when she used it. Lee Anne, however, thinks aggression is wrong. So she felt an emotional charge when Kelly mentioned aggression. She was the one judging.*

You will be bothered by the guilt that you see reflected in others only as long as the guilt in your mind is real to you. As you detach from the personal thought system in your mind you will merely observe without an emotional charge that others feel guilty.

*Sherman was listening to his friend, Martin, go off on the actions of certain politicians. Martin was giving off a lot of angry energy but Sherman rested in peace within himself. He could see that Martin was projecting guilt. But because he felt no guilt himself he was unaffected by Martin's words or energy. When Martin seemed to want a reaction Sherman calmly stated, "You seem to be very upset by this." Martin felt that he was heard and understood, which was what he needed at that moment.*

As you learn that guilt has no real basis you may judge against yourself when you do feel guilt. You may feel guilty for feeling guilty! This only means that guilt is still real to you. It is not enough to read that guilt is not real. You must truly learn that guilt is not real to release it. This happens as you grow your awareness of Truth and undo the many ways in which you believe in guilt. You will know that you have released guilt when you observe others and yourself without judgment.

You do have to make choices in the world. So you do have to make judgments. But these are judgments based on what is practically useful, not projections of absolute-moral meaning. When you are making a judgment based on the facts at hand you do not have an emotional charge.

*Jessica needs a new car. She doesn't look at a car as an extension of herself. She doesn't need it to make her happy or to give her status. She just needs one to get around. So she is not emotional about the car. She makes a list of what she needs and wants in a car and she is willing to compromise on her wants.*

20. Guilt and responsibility

You may feel that it is irresponsible to not feel guilty. You may feel that guilt or the fear of guilt is what motivates you to be responsible. But remember that the personal thought system is validated by guilt. The source of your guilt is your belief that it is real. And your guilt prevents you from looking inward, finding Truth, and releasing the personal thought system. So it is clear why the personal thought system thinks it is irresponsible for you to not feel guilty!

Actually, guilt interferes with you accepting responsibility. Instead of responding to facts you respond to projections of absolute-moral meaning.

*Clark's hours at work were cut and he hasn't been paying his child support. He feels that this makes him a bad father rather than just a man in a hard situation. He could go to his ex-wife and make arrangements to pay less now and more when his income goes up. But he can't cope with the guilt and shame that he feels in this situation. So he ignores her calls, texts, and emails. And she feels forced to take him to court.*

When you feel guilty you confuse *responsibility* with *blame*. So you find it difficult to accept responsibility. You may project your self-blame outward onto another or others, missing opportunities to find guilt in your mind and release it. You make yourself a victim.

*Annie was discussing her poor relationships with men with her long-time friend, DeWitt. When DeWitt pointed out to Annie that she chose emotionally distant men like her father for partners she became angry and defensive. Because of unconscious guilt in her mind she felt that DeWitt was blaming her for others treating her poorly. But DeWitt was merely pointing out a pattern in Annie's life that he had observed. He was seeking to empower her by making her aware of for what she was responsible in her relationships so that she could undo the pattern.*

*John is obese. He has been diagnosed with diabetes, high blood pressure, and heart disease. His doctor explained to him that his weight is the cause of or at least contributes greatly to these illnesses. She told him this so that he can take control of his own health by changing his diet and losing weight. But in his guilt John feels blamed. Eating to excess is the way that he deals with bad feelings. So he binges after seeing the doctor and decides to not go to her anymore.*

*Violet is very critical. When her children became adults they chose to limit their interactions with her. When she asks her daughter Wendy why they avoid her Wendy tells her honestly that she is very critical of their lives and choices. It is hard for them to be around someone who seems so unhappy with them. But Violet hears Wendy's honest explanation as blame. She feels Wendy is attacking her. So instead of hearing her daughter and choosing to look at her own critical nature Violet only becomes more resentful of her children.*

In extreme cases, unconscious but crushing guilt shows up as the total inability to accept responsibility. For such individuals anything that does not go right in their lives is *always* someone else's fault. Even in a guilty world this is recognized as pathological (narcissistic personality disorder, antisocial personality disorder, etc.).

Guilt can result in you taking responsibility where you are not responsible.

*Brenda has been studying metaphysical teachings about attracting and manifesting. She has come to believe that on some level she chooses everything that shows up in form. Brenda does not live in an area where tornadoes usually occur. But her neighborhood and home were hit by a freak tornado. Now she is digging around in her mind trying to find out why she chose this disaster. She sees the tornado as bad, not as meaningless. She does not consciously think that she is blaming herself. She thinks that she is trying to take responsibility so she does not make another disaster happen. But what she really seeks is how to control her mind so that she will not make other "bad" forms show up. She does not want to be guilty for another disaster again.*

Guilt also leads to you taking responsibility where others are responsible.

*Giselle feels that she has no right to be happy as long as anyone else in the world is suffering. Unconsciously she feels that it is her responsibility to make others whole and happy.*

*Stephen is a white man who is generally liberal in his political views. He has friends and acquaintances of many different races. But when someone of a different color brings up racial inequality he gets irritated. He argues to himself that things have changed greatly and even though there are still some problems racial minorities need to get over what he sees as their attachment to victimhood. But his irritation indicates that he feels guilty. Even though he has never actively played a part in oppressing racial minorities he unconsciously feels guilty for what he unconsciously sees as his privileged position in society.*

*Whenever Margo's wife, Lydia, shares a problem with her Margo feels stressed. She projects her own guilt into Lydia's situations. So she feels that she has to fix Lydia's problems. But Lydia is not asking her to fix her problems. She is just discussing them. When Margo jumps in with her ideas of how to fix a situation, Lydia feels that Margo doesn't think she can take care of herself. Margo feels burdened by Lydia's problems and Lydia feels disrespected. Lydia stops sharing her problems with Margo and Margo feels shut out.*

When you take responsibility that belongs to another it is *co-dependency.* You enable others to stay in their immaturity, illness, or dysfunction.

*Ricardo did his best to raise his 4 children in a typical middle-class family. But alcoholism runs in his family. His son, Carlos, and his daughter, Lisa, became involved with drugs and alcohol in high school. They both became addicted. Ricardo is crushed by guilt for passing on "bad" genes and for possible mistakes that he made as a father. Carlos and Lisa know what they have to do to get well but they are not yet willing to get well. They have both been in and out of 12-step programs and expensive rehabilitation facilities for which Ricardo paid. Ricardo is always running to rescue them. His other relationships suffer and he is nearly broke. He unconsciously enables Carlos and Lisa to stay in their disease by not giving them the opportunity to hit bottom and willingly seek help for themselves.*

Ricardo not only enables his adult children. He does not deal with guilt at its actual source, within himself. His co-dependency is actually a defense against releasing guilt from his own mind. By focusing on his children's problems he avoids his own. This is irresponsible, not responsible.

When guilt and the fear of punishment that it inspires are unconscious you respond to them in dysfunctional, irresponsible, and sometimes risky ways.

*Craig was raised in a strict Christian home where he was taught that homosexuality is a sin. Craig is homosexual but he repressed his attraction to men and married a woman and had a family. But when he is under stress he finds it difficult to resist his attraction to men. In his guilt he can hardly acknowledge this. So he meets with strangers in dark places for quick, anonymous sex that he tries to forget about later. Because each time he vows it will be the last time he does not carry condoms for protection against sexually transmitted diseases. So if his anonymous partners do not have condoms they have unprotected sex. In his guilty denial Craig puts himself, his wife, and his male sexual partners at risk.*

*To deal with her unconscious guilt Rachel became an over-achiever. She married and had children, but her relationships suffer because she is always too pre-occupied with succeeding at work to attend to them. She feels that her failing relationships are her "fault", but she does nothing to change the situation. She blames herself and feels more guilt rather than takes responsibility and deals with the guilt that drives her to over-achieve. Her guilt over her failed relationships drives her further into her work.*

*Birth control pills make Danielle ill. For her, guilt shows up as low self-worth. When a new boyfriend wanted to have sex without a condom she explained that she was not on birth control. He wanted to take the risk and because she was afraid of losing him she acquiesced. She ended up pregnant with a child that neither wanted nor could afford to raise.*

*When Brandt was very young he was partly responsible for the death of a friend. Since then he has unconsciously felt that he deserves death. At first he was drawn to risky activities like racing, mountain climbing, and parachuting to dance with death. But the adrenaline rush from these activities gave him a boost of endorphins that acted like a drug to numb the pain he felt from unconscious guilt. So now risky activities serve two purposes for him: to temporarily relieve pain as he tempts death to take him.*

When you feel too guilty to take responsibility for your life you may martyr yourself on your own choices.

*Because of unconscious guilt Ophelia keeps herself busy. She cannot let her mind rest because she is afraid to look inward. Though busy-ness is her choice, she acts as though she is put-upon by all of her responsibilities. She plays the martyr. And because she cannot rest her health suffers. She makes herself a martyr of that as well.*

When you release guilt you stop confusing responsibility with blame. You take responsibility because you recognize that to be responsible is to be empowered.

*Nancy has been growing her awareness of Truth for many years. An effect of this has been her willingness to take responsibility for her life in the world. She used to have low self-esteem and allowed others to disrespect and mistreat her. But she was guided by the Teacher of Truth to get into therapy and deal with her low self-worth. Eventually she learned to set boundaries with others. This has transformed her life for the better. Some unhealthy relationships fell away when she no longer played the doormat. But they have been replaced by healthy, loving, respectful relationships.*

You will read more about how releasing guilt leads to you being responsible in part 27.

## Releasing Guilt

21. The world as a useful mirror

You are in pain and conflict because you are not in your natural state of limitless Being. And what holds you in this unnatural state of limitation is the guilt that maintains your belief in it. So if you want freedom and peace you do not need the world to change. You only need to release the guilt in your mind.

You may think that the way to peace is to take yourself off to a cave somewhere to spend your life in quiet contemplation. But that could be a way to denial. You need the world to mirror your mind back to you to learn if your peace is complete. If you are ever upset by the world then your peace is not complete.

*Larry is at peace when he is home studying spiritual teachings and meditating. But as soon as he steps out the door and interacts with the world his peace disappears. He finds that he is emotionally charged by the world. This is because he still unconsciously believes in guilt. And interacting with the world is what brings this to his awareness.*

You attain peace faster when you are conscious of your belief in guilt because only then can you release it. And you bring your belief in guilt to your conscious awareness by paying attention to your emotional responses to the world. So you do not need to dig around in your mind for your every thought of guilt and fear. These will come up naturally as you go about life in the world.

This is not a comfortable process! You will look directly at the false ideas within your own mind which hold up the world of conflict that you seem to see outside of you. And your belief in the guilt in your mind will make you turn condemnation on yourself at first. The personal thought system will also be very resistant. But you will accept its resistance as your own only to the degree to which you believe that you are guilty. As you experience the peace that comes from releasing guilt your resistance will fall away.

You have only two choices while you perceive yourself in a world. You can stay in pain and conflict, denying that their source is within you, feeling like a powerless victim of a guilty world, and numbing yourself against them. This will not release pain and conflict from your mind. Or you can look directly at the false ideas that are the source of your pain and conflict so that you can release them. This will lead you out of pain and conflict. Either way is painful. But the former way you will remain in pain. And the latter way will lead you out of pain to peace.

## 22. From guilt to Truth

Guilt is the fabric of the personal thought system because guilt is what makes it seem real to you. You cannot identify with a self and not experience guilt. And if you experience guilt you must be identified with a self. The only way out of guilt is to release the personal thought system from your mind. And since guilt is what holds it in place you must release guilt to do this. If the personal thought system is the cross on which you crucify yourself guilt is what nails you to the cross.

You do not have to worry that you will suddenly drop the personal thought system and its world and be in Truth. The contrast between the limited personal experience and limitless Truth would be too shocking for your mind. Instead, as you release guilt you will slowly make a transition to a thought system of Truth (Teacher of Truth) that bridges limitation and Limitlessness. You will still seem to be in a world but you will be aware that the Truth is true. So for a while you will seem to have two realities. But as your awareness of Truth grows you will detach more and more from the limited personal experience. And when you finally do drop the self it will be the most natural thing to do because you will know that *only* the Truth is true.

You must have some awareness that the Truth is true to begin the process of releasing guilt. Only one experience of Truth is enough to show you that there is an experience other than the limited personal experience. The reality and value of a single experience of Truth is compelling. It will transform you.

*Rich had been reading various spiritual teachings for a couple of years. He thought he understood them. Then one day as he was out for a walk contemplating some of the ideas he'd been reading he had a moment of incredible clarity where he knew, really knew, that the Truth is true. It was only a moment but he was transformed. What he had been reading was true! There really is another experience. Now he more fully understands what he reads. And during his meditations he recalls his experience of Truth to remind himself to What he wants to open himself. Just that one experience showed him that peace is possible.*

*Abigail had attended church off and on all her life. She was not particularly religious or spiritual. Church was more of a cultural experience for her. One day while at work the world disappeared for a moment. She experienced formless, boundlessness, and incredible Love. Since that experience she has been reading various spiritual teachings to understand it. She now knows What is Real and possible. This gives her a measure of peace.*

*Kirk was a glider pilot who experienced a terrible crash. His body was crushed and he nearly died. When he awakened from a coma he remembered an experience of an incredible Light that embodied boundless Love to him. He knows that It was real and true. Now he spends much time contemplating It and bringing It into greater awareness through meditation. His awareness brings him peace.*

Your awareness of Truth grows slowly at first because guilt is so real to you. Guilt makes you feel unworthy of Truth. Guilt makes you fear Truth because you confuse It with a god. You fear that Truth wants to punish you. You fear that Truth demands your total sacrifice. So while one experience of Truth is enough to begin the process to peace, it is not enough to bring you total peace. Your belief in guilt and fear will pull you back to the personal thought system again and again. It may be uncomfortable but you do not fear it as you do Truth.

*Hailey notices that every period of peace is followed by a longer period of darkness and pain. She's afraid that she is failing on her spiritual path. But she is simply drawn to guilt and fear because unconsciously she still believes that they are real.*

You may think that your vacillations between peace and conflict are a failure. But they are the process of learning to wholly trust Truth. So when guilt comes up it is an opportunity to bring it to the Teacher of Truth in your mind to release the thoughts behind it. You will release guilt and grow your awareness of Truth at the same time. And as Truth becomes true for you, you will release guilt faster and easier.

*Bertrand has been releasing guilt for many years. His belief in a punishing god has come up in many different forms and from many different angles. He has often had to sit with the contrast between his loving experiences of Truth and his concept of a punishing god. But now this belief is mostly undone. When guilt arises he releases it quickly in the awareness that it has no basis. The Truth is untouched by anything that seems to happen in form. There is no punishing god. Only the Truth is True.*

23. Looking at personal guilt

Unconscious and conscious feelings of inadequacy, unworthiness, and fear of punishment are manifestations of unconscious guilt. They are the personal experience. For everyone this plays out through their personal story. This lens of personal guilt is what you must look at first.

*Rocko's father was highly critical of Rocko. Because of the guilt in his personal thought system Rocko accepted the message from his father that he is inherently inadequate. As an adult he never feels that he is good enough or has done enough for others. He seeks others' approval but even when they give it he does not accept it. His unconscious story for himself is that he will never be good enough; he will never have done enough to make up for his intrinsic guilt.*

*Carlotta's mother told her often when she was a child that she did not want her. Carlotta felt like a burden to her mother, which is how guilt manifested for her. But Carlotta learned when she was twelve that certain men wanted her. She began then to trade sex for a temporary feeling of worth. Her personal story is that her only value is in the sex she provides to men.*

*When he was a young boy Peter's brother was killed in an accident that Peter survived. The guilt in Peter's mind manifested as survivors guilt. Peter had done nothing to cause the accident or his brother's death. He felt guilt just for surviving. After high school Peter joined the army. He eagerly went off to war because unconsciously he was hoping to die the death he felt he had cheated before. When his unit was ambushed some of his comrades were killed. Peter was physically wounded but survived. But psychologically his guilt crushed him and he had a breakdown. His illogical personal story is that he killed his brother and comrades. He should not be alive.*

All feelings are caused by unconscious or conscious thoughts. When you are triggered emotionally you can look at the thoughts behind your feelings to find the guilt. At first you are not likely to be able to do this when the triggers occur. But you can look at them later when your emotions have cooled down.

*Rocko has found just enough self-worth to want inner peace. He has allowed Truth to come into his awareness. This led him to study various psycho-spiritual teachings. He has learned that his relationships are very stressful because he is co-dependent. He has learned to look at what occurs within himself when he feels an urge to take responsibility for others. He realizes that he is trying to compensate for feelings of inadequacy. He has traced this feeling back to his childhood with his father.*

You may need professional counseling with a therapist or spiritual teacher to help you look at your personal story for guilt. But keep in mind that traditional counseling seeks to validate the self, not help you to release your identification with it. You can use traditional counseling temporarily, however, to help you to examine your story and its effects on your life. And it may give you tools for releasing some of your false beliefs.

*Ashley's parents were addicted to drama. They were wrapped up in themselves, each other, their dysfunctional friends, and their mutual drama to the exclusion of their children. Their children were little more than cute accessories in their lives. As the eldest, Ashley took on the role of care-taker for her younger siblings. She grew up feeling responsible for everyone around her. As an adult she got into therapy and joined a 12-step program for co-dependents. Through these she learned that she was still playing her childhood role of care-taker for others. She also learned that she is no longer responsible for others. Her time as care-taker was over as soon as her youngest sibling became an adult.*

Guilt comes disguised in many forms. All negative emotions can ultimately be traced back to guilt.

Depression = anger = fear = guilt

Depression is anger turned inward. So when you are depressed ask yourself why you are angry.

*Ezra had been depressed for a couple of days. He finally decided he needed to trace back to when the depression started. He realized it began when his son told him he was joining the army instead of going to college. He's angry because he feels that the army is a waste of his son's intellect.*

As was noted in part 6, anger is a defensive response. It indicates fear. So when you are angry ask yourself why you are afraid.

*Ezra dug deeper and realized that he fears for his son's future. And he fears for his son's life. What if there is another war?*

Fear indicates guilt. So when you are afraid, ask yourself why you feel guilty.

*Beyond his fear for his son's future Ezra feels fear because of his own guilt. His family was not military but he was raised in a military community. Many of his friends served. Ezra realizes that he has always felt guilty for not serving. So at the heart of his depression is guilt for not having chosen to serve in the military.*

*After he realized this Ezra's depression lifted. As an adult he can see that he has served his community and country as a university professor. While he is still concerned for his son, his anger over his son's career choice has dissipated. Ezra finds he is able to support him.*

The personal self is limited, imperfect, and self-centered. Every personal story is littered with stories of violations of social-morality.

*When she was using drugs Mitzi used and manipulated people to get drugs, to give her money, to take care of her, etc. She is clean now but she carries a lot of conscious guilt for these actions.*

Sometimes you will release guilt for specific actions or inactions as soon as you bring them to conscious awareness.

*In therapy Hideki discovered that he was unconsciously holding onto guilt for accidently breaking his brother's nose when they were wrestling as teenagers. An adult and a father now, as soon as this story for guilt came up he laughed it off as just one of those things that happen with kids.*

The personal thought system points to your violations of social-morality to "prove" your intrinsic guilt. So there is value in making amends when possible. It strips away the top layer of guilt.

*As part of her 12-step program of recovery from drug addiction Mitzi wrote down everything for which she felt guilty. Where possible, she contacted people to make verbal or financial amends. Going forward, the personal thought system in her mind could no longer prod her with these stories. She could say and mean, "I made mistakes. I made amends for them. It's over."*

*Scott regretted how cruel he was to Lena during their divorce. Whenever he was reminded of his behavior during that time he felt sick to his stomach. Years later he mentioned this to a friend who advised him to apologize to Lena for his own sake. So Scott contacted her and apologized. She was cold to him but he did feel better for having made the amends. His past behavior no longer tormented him.*

The personal thought system points to your personal story and your violations of social-morality to explain your feelings of guilt. This validates the personal identity. It also keeps you from looking deeper for the real cause of your feelings of guilt.

24. Releasing the personal thought system

The central belief of the personal thought system is that it is real because it killed Truth and replaced It. When you identify with a self you unconsciously believe that this is true for you. So you unconsciously feel intrinsically guilty, unworthy, and inadequate. Your personal stories for guilt give shape to these feelings. And guilt hijacks your social conscience to add to these feelings.

Making amends for violations of social-morality removes stories from your mind to which the personal thought system can point to justify your feelings of guilt. But this only releases the stories, not the guilt. You cannot be without an identity. So you will only release guilt when the Truth is true for you. Because only then will you release the personal thought system.

To summarize how to grow your awareness of Truth:

The 4 habits for inner peace: commune with Truth daily, turn within to Truth throughout the day, call on the Teacher of Truth for guidance, and allow Love to extend through your mind to learn that you are Love.

Do not trust guilt and fear. They do not tell you the truth about yourself. When fear arises to block your awareness of Truth look with the Teacher of Truth at your unconscious and conscious beliefs in guilt. Question them. Remember that guilt is a misinterpretation of your discomfort identifying with a self. Your discomfort is a sign that you are not aware of Truth. So turn your mind away from guilt and fear and turn it inward to Truth.

Remember your experiences of Truth. They show you that Truth is not dead. Truth is whole and intact. It is not touched by the self, its story, or its world. Your identification with a self only blocks your *awareness* of Truth. And since Truth is untouched by the self there is no basis for guilt.

Compare your loving, peaceful experiences of Truth with the concept of a punishing god outside of you. Notice how you experience Truth now but "God" is something that you are supposed to experience in the future. A present experience is real. An idea projected into the future is not.

The personal stories that give shape to guilt in your mind are woven into your personal identity. So you will not release those stories until you begin to release your identification with a self.

*Megan was neglected in her childhood and has spent years in therapy dealing with her feelings of unworthiness. She learned that her childhood experiences gave shape to her bad feelings about herself. She learned to undo some of the thoughts of unworthiness that made her life a mess. But her whole identity was wrapped up in being a victim of neglectful parents. She was not able to forgive them.*

As the Truth becomes true for you the premise for guilt begins to be undone in your mind. And forgiving (releasing) happens naturally.

*Megan had an experience of Truth. She learned to meditate to grow her awareness of Truth. She invited the Teacher of Truth into her awareness and in time her trust in Truth grew. One day she realized that she didn't see herself as a victim anymore. She realized that she never was a victim. It is true that her parents neglected her as a child, but they did not cause her feelings of unworthiness. Their neglect only validated her sense of intrinsic unworthiness. Megan doesn't forgive her parents because she doesn't need to. She released (forgave) her personal story of victimhood and is at peace.*

You do not have to seek out every possible form that your unconscious belief in guilt takes or can take in your mind. In fact if you are tempted to do this it is the personal thought system trying to take over the process to reinforce guilt, not to release it. It will be happy to make up as many stories for guilt as it can!

*Ian has learned that unconscious guilt is an obstacle to peace. Instead of dealing with guilt as it comes up he spends a lot of time trying to remember every incident in his life where he could possibly have felt guilty. He is now not sure if he remembers some things correctly. It's as though he is seeing guilt that he did not feel before. And he feels like his guilt fills a bottom-less pit that he will never empty.*

As you go about your life your unconscious belief in guilt will rise to your conscious awareness naturally. You do not have to force the process. In fact, much that you believe unconsciously will be undone unconsciously as the Truth becomes true for you. Your mind will generalize and see similarities between stories, releasing guilt of which you are not even aware.

The personal thought system will not change. Guilt is its fabric and projection is the way that it thinks. But as the Truth becomes true for you, you will realize that you can observe the personal thought system. And since you can observe it, it is not you. As you detach from it you will hear it but you will not listen to it.

*Brody noticed that as soon as anyone walks into the room the personal thought system in his mind makes judgments on them. He's learned to let these thoughts happen and then to let them go as he turns within and remembers that only the Truth is true.*

*Ellen lost her job and the bills are piling up. The personal thought system in her mind is full of panicky thoughts. It is using her situation to draw her attention back to it. So she sits with her frightening thoughts. She feels the expectation of punishment behind them and realizes that this comes from a belief in intrinsic guilt. So she turns to the still, quiet of Truth within her mind. The Truth is with her. She is not guilty. And now she knows that she will be guided to do what needs to be done to take care of the self in the world.*

When you are detached from the personal thought system you learn that it always speaks for itself. It never speaks for you:

It must believe in guilt to believe that it exists. But *your* existence is in Truth, not in guilt. Guilt blocks your awareness of Truth.

It fears death because deep down it knows that it is not real and that you can release it. Your releasing it is not "death" exactly but to the personal thought system there is no difference between "dying" and you withdrawing your attention from it. But in Truth *you* have no beginning or ending.

It is limited, insecure, and vulnerable. But in Truth *you* are Limitless, Whole, and Inviolate.

When you are tempted to listen to the personal thought system turn what it says back on it. Then remember your experiences of Truth. This will help you to release it even further.

25. Accepting not-Truth as it is

As long as you identify with a self you will unconsciously and consciously believe that guilt is real. You will not accept that the self is inherently imperfect and limited. You will judge the personal thought system's thoughts. You will judge the self's attitudes and behavior. You will feel driven to perfect the self to mitigate guilt. You will try to be a "good" self. And you will respond to your guilt inappropriately and ineffectively, resulting in a dysfunctional life for the self and adding to your guilt.

As long as you identify with a self you will unconsciously project away the guilt that you unconsciously believe is real in you. So you will not accept that other selves are imperfect and limited. You will judge them for their dysfunctions because theirs mirrors yours. And you will want to fix them instead of yourself.

As long as you identify with a self you will fight against natural and human laws because you will project onto them the cause of your experience of limitation.

It is the same to fight against not-Truth as to embrace it. Either approach means you think that it is real and makes it more real to you. But as the Truth becomes true for you, you will detach from the self and its thought system. You will know that it is not you. Your releasing it shows up as you accepting it as it is, without judgment.

*Alisha was a perfectionist. She was hard on herself and those around her. But she has become aware of Truth and with this awareness she has accepted that the self will never be perfect. Because she is aware of Perfection within she no longer needs to seek for It in the self. When she makes inevitable mistakes now she easily makes correction or amends or laughs them off. When others make mistakes she easily accepts their correction or amends and she forgets about it. She is much lighter.*

Your acceptance of the self with which you identify will extend to other selves. To accept others means that you allow them to be without resisting them. It means that you realize that you cannot change them. It means that you just observe them without projecting absolute-moral meaning onto their behavior.

*For years Gwen railed against any form of cruelty that she saw in the world. She saw cruelty as wrong. As an imperfect human she was sometimes cruel so when she saw cruelty in the world it triggered her guilt. She went around angry with the world much of the time. But she has found Truth and peace and now she accepts that the self is not her so it does not need to be perfect. Because she has accepted this about the self with which she identifies she has accepted that others are not perfect and never will be. If she feels an emotional charge about someone else's behavior she quickly remembers that only the Truth is True and Perfect. The emotional charge dissipates and she is at peace again.*

To accept someone does not mean that you like them. Nor does it mean that you do not set boundaries with others. It does mean that you are able to respond without an emotional charge.

*Ralph's uncle Jeb is a bitter, critical man. No one in the family likes him but because he is family he is invited to holiday events. Since Ralph has become aware of Truth and found peace within himself, his feelings toward Jeb have gone from hating him to barely tolerating him to feeling compassion for him. But Ralph still does not like Jeb. And when Jeb says something inappropriate or hurtful to someone at a family gathering in Ralph's home Ralph lets Jeb know that his welcome has a boundary. If Jeb cannot be polite in the future he will not be invited to family events in Ralph's home.*

*Chris has worked his whole career in a small company where nepotism has played a large role in who got a promotion. Chris is not related to the owner and he has been passed over for promotion twice so that the positions for which he was qualified could go to unqualified relatives of his boss. For many years Chris burned about his work situation. He stayed because he liked his job and his co-workers. But as he has grown aware of Truth and finds fulfillment within he has no need to ask anything from the world. He has come to accept that his work situation is not wrong or bad. It is just the way it is. After he was passed over for promotion the second time Chris chose to move on.*

As Truth becomes true for you your acceptance of not-Truth will also extend to nature and to social boundaries.

*Noette realized that climate changes were causing more floods in her city. Because she is aware of Truth she does not see this as wrong or bad. She sees this as just a fact. This gives her the clarity of mind to see her choices without judgment. She can stay where she is without flood insurance, stay where she is with flood insurance, or she can move to higher ground.*

*Dale used to rail against any form of government. But since he has become aware of Truth he accepts that government is a fact of life in the world. He still thinks some regulations and laws are excessive and he continues to work to change them. But he no longer gets upset by them. He realizes that the world will always be imperfect. It is also temporary and passing.*

You cannot force yourself to accept not-Truth as it is. As long as it is real to you, you will believe that guilt is real. So you will feel a need to judge and to change not-Truth.

*For Melinda the Truth is a nice idea that she has read about in spiritual books. It is not a real experience for her. But the world is very real to her. She is emotionally charged often, every day. She feels like a victim in her relationships with others. She sees a world of victimizers and victims. She belongs to various political and social organizations that work to make the world a "better place". She tries to forgive others because she thinks she "should". But she really cannot yet. First she will have to grow her awareness of Truth.*

Acceptance will come naturally to you as the Truth becomes true for you. Acceptance will be the *signal* that the Truth has become true for you.

26. True forgiving and true compassion

In your personal identity you have many stories of guilt for you and for others. You may think that you have a lot to forgive. But all that you really have to forgive is your belief in guilt.

Your belief in guilt shows up as your belief in the self's stories as your reality. You hold onto these stories because they define you as a self. But as you grow the Truth in your awareness you find your wholeness in the present with Truth. Truth replaces the self's stories as your reality.

*Eppie was raped by an acquaintance. It left her emotionally scarred and mistrustful of everyone. For many years being a victim of rape was part of her identity. Through therapy she changed her identity to survivor of rape. Eventually she invited Truth into her awareness. As her awareness of Truth grew she let go of rape as part of her identity. It is a fact that rape occurred in her personal story. But she no longer identifies with the story. The rape has become a distant memory without an emotional charge.*

Since all that you really have to forgive is your belief in guilt you cannot truly forgive from the personal thought system. True forgiving is the natural effect of knowing that the Truth is true. You realize that the Truth is untouched by anything that the self seems to do or to not do. So you understand that there is nothing to forgive.

*Zander was a small child and he was often bullied. He became defined by his insecurities and his victimhood as he grew up. He carried this persona into adulthood. In middle age he experienced Truth and he spent many years growing his awareness of Truth. Eventually he realized that he gave absolute-moral meaning to and defined himself by those childhood experiences. He realizes now that it is nothing but a story in his mind about himself. It is not real. He has let it go.*

As the Truth becomes True for you, you will first forgive yourself. Then forgiveness will extend to others.

*Chandra used to be very hard on herself. She remembered her every violation of social-morality from her childhood to the present. She was also very hard on others and never forgot what she felt was an offense against her. But the Truth has become true for her and she has released a lot of guilt. She now sees her past mistakes as only mistakes. She is quick to forgive herself when she makes a mistake now. And she also sees other's mistakes as only mistakes. She accepts others' amends and forgives easily because she never feels an offense has occurred.*

*Mary Margaret was raised a Roman Catholic. She left the Church as a teenager but she spent much of her adult life blaming the Church for her feelings of guilt. But as Truth has grown in her awareness she has released a lot of guilt. She has learned about inherent guilt in the personal thought system. Now she feels compassion for those in her former Church. They believe that guilt is real. She knows how much pain they are in because she used to believe in guilt, too.*

When you are aware of Truth and guilt is being released from your mind you live in a different world than you did before. You live in a forgiven world. You do not see it as wrong or bad. You do not give it absolute-moral meaning. You observe it without an emotional charge.

When you are aware of Truth you do observe that the world is made up of selves who are dysfunctional when they are not aware of Truth. You observe that they are in pain and that they respond ineffectively and inappropriately to their pain. You know that their responses to pain are all the same. Their seeming differences are a matter of scale.

*When Juliet is feeling guilty and frightened she lashes out at those around her.*

*When Harvey is guilty and frightened he drinks himself into oblivion.*

*When Sinclair is guilty and frightened he sets off bombs in public places.*

When you know that the Truth is True your attitude toward the world is true compassion. You first feel compassion toward yourself.

*When Chandra remembers how hard she used to be on herself she only feels compassion for her former self. She realizes that she believed that she was wrong and bad. She felt guilty and afraid.*

*Pascal has been clean and sober for fifteen years. He used to hate the manipulative, abusive man he was when he was using drugs and alcohol. But since the Truth has become true for him he remembers that man with compassion. He realizes that he was sick, not bad.*

True compassion is the natural result of true forgiveness. You see that others suffer but you know that their suffering is not real. You see that it is caused by their mistaken thoughts. But you also see that they do not yet know this.

*Ari watched as the marriage of his sister and brother-in-law deteriorated. He watched each ask the other to make them whole. And when they couldn't do this for each other they projected guilt onto each other. He suggested counseling years ago and they went. They learned how to communicate without blaming the other. But they only changed the way that they communicated. They still really blamed the other. Neither wanted to work on their underlying stories, which drove them to project guilt for their unhappiness. Now Ari watches as they go through a messy, contentious divorce. He knows that each is causing his or her own suffering. And he feels compassion for both because they do not know this. Mostly, he feels compassion for both because neither thinks that they are worth the effort to become aware of Truth and be at peace.*

True compassion is dispassionate because it is not personal. It comes from the awareness that the Truth is true. If you feel emotional about another's story you identify with them as a self. So guilt is real to you, not Truth.

*Ari's peace is not disturbed watching his sister and brother-in-law go through their divorce. He knows that only the Truth is True. He knows for them that only the Truth within their minds is True. He knows that they are safe and whole in Truth even though they are not aware of this.*

When you are truly compassionate you see no difference between perpetrators and seeming-victims. You see that both are in pain. The perpetrator projects guilt, chooses to see themselves as a victim of guilty others, and lashes out against them. And the seeming-victim projects guilt and chooses to see themselves as a victim of the perpetrator.

Your compassion comes from understanding because the personal thought system in your mind has played both roles, too.

*When Glen heard about the bombing it was to him just more of the same of what the world is about. Unless they are aware of Truth everyone is in pain and is acting out from that pain. He used to be the same way. But now, without guilt in his mind, he has no motivation to project absolute-moral meaning onto the situation. It was not wrong or bad. It was nothing. But he is aware that those involved do not see it as nothing. So he feels the same compassion for the perpetrators as the seeming-victims. He knows that the perpetrators felt like victims first. They projected guilt onto others so they blew them up. He knows that, unless they are aware of Truth, the seeming-victims are projecting guilt onto the perpetrators. They are choosing to suffer. He pities them all in their unnecessary pain.*

You cannot force true forgiving or true compassion. True forgiving is the natural effect of knowing that the Truth is true. And true compassion is the natural effect of true forgiving. Both come naturally as you release guilt and grow your awareness of Truth.

*Kera heard Glen tell someone else that he felt compassion for both the bombers and the seeming-victims. He sees only people in pain all around: the bombers, those injured, the families of the dead and injured, and the people of the city where the bombing occurred. This infuriates Kera, who sees the bombers as guilty and everyone else as their victims. As a citizen of the nation where the bombing occurred, she, too, feels like a victim. She and Glen are viewing the same event but having completely different experiences. Kera projects unconscious guilt and fear and experiences fear and anger. She lives in a frightening world of pain and conflict. Glen sees others' pain but feels detachment and dispassionate compassion. He lives in a real world of peace from which he observes a false world of pain.*

27. A conscious life

The self is an effect of your mind. It is an idea in your mind. Its life is shaped by your unconscious and conscious beliefs. Your beliefs determine the self's attitudes, behavior, choices, and energy. These determine its relationship to the world around it.

You couldn't cope with a full awareness of the guilt in your mind. So when guilt is real to you, you spend the self's life responding to unconscious guilt and the fear that it inspires. You do not understand what motivates you. You feel powerless. You cannot see how you make the self's life. You live unconsciously.

*Cassidy feels her life is out of control. She is about to go through her second divorce in two years. She has been laid off. Her home is in foreclosure. She has a heap of debt and has to file for bankruptcy. Her first husband is still fighting for custody of their children. She is anxious and has panic attacks. But Cassidy has so much guilt in her mind that she cannot look honestly at how she has made this life for herself through a series of choices motivated from unconscious guilt and fear. Sometimes she expresses to others that she thinks her life is such a mess because she is inherently bad. She thinks she is being punished. When others try to point out her choices she cannot see facts because in her guilt she confuses responsibility with blame. She goes to her doctor to get drugs instead of a referral to a therapist. And her doctor, in his guilt, cannot say no. He knows better but he gives her prescriptions for anxiety and depression so that he does not feel guilty about letting her down.*

An unconscious life is one where you project guilt. You turn yourself into a powerless victim of a cruel world.

*Ivan is on his third divorce. In his mind all women are grasping bitches and marriage is a financial money-pit. When others point out that each time he married the same kind of gold-digging woman he lashes out at them. Any hint that he may be partly responsible for how his life is turning out brings up so much unconscious guilt that he gets terrified. And fear makes him angry and defensive. Now he is their victim, too. He would rather be a victim than look at from where his choices in life come so he can learn to make better choices.*

When guilt is real to you it is difficult for you to be in the present because unconscious guilt is in the present. So your mind is elsewhere. You live in memories or projections of the future. Or you dwell on things that are simply not here. These thoughts, too, may contain guilt. And you experience the guilt now. But you have the illusion that the guilt is not here. It is in the past, the future, or elsewhere. And since the guilt does not seem to be here you feel that you cannot do anything about it.

*When her mind isn't occupied with something else Dakota replays her mother's various criticisms and digs over the years. She dwells in a story of being her mother's victim. Even though Dakota is experiencing feelings of guilt and resentment now, she sees their source in the past. She feels she cannot do anything about them. She does not see that her present thoughts are the source of her present feelings.*

*Whenever Pindar's mind has a quiet moment it runs on fantasies of future success or future disaster, depending on his mood. If he is in a good mood he fantasizes about success. When he feels down or guilty he seems unable to help imagining future disaster. Because of unconscious guilt in his mind he finds it impossible to be in the present.*

*Tim considers himself a spiritual person. He tries to meditate but he cannot because his mind dwells on the various injustices he sees in the world. He feels powerless so he ends up enraged rather than peaceful. He does not see that he obsesses on the seeming-injustices that happen to others because he does not want to face his thoughts about the seeming-injustices in his own life.*

When your life is unconscious you have accidents, you fumble your responsibilities, you miss opportunities, and you cannot hear the Teacher of Truth's guidance.

*Ron was recently reminded of a painful experience in his past. He does not want to consciously think about it. But he finds that he bangs into things, trips over things, and knocks things over. His mind is pre-occupied with unconscious thoughts about the past experience.*

*Candy keeps herself so busy to avoid quiet time that she has the reputation of being chronically late.*

*Jim's boss wasn't supposed to let anyone know that there would soon be a position opening for which Jim would be qualified. But he dropped some hints to Jim that Jim missed because his mind chronically dwells on questions of his performance in his current position.*

*Robin has been on a spiritual path for many years. She has read many books and been to many seminars. She can recite lines from the spiritual books she reads. She feels that these mean that she has given her life to the Teacher of Truth. So she does not understand why she is not at peace.*

*Robin is not at peace because her mind is anywhere but in the present with Truth. She does not want to look at her thoughts with the Teacher of Truth. So she waits passively and unconsciously for It to somehow mysteriously fix her life without her.*

Trying to be present to the Truth within you brings up guilt. But as you work through the guilt you find that you can be present more and more. When you are present to Truth you are also mindful of what is going on around you. You live consciously.

Without guilt you do not blame or judge yourself or others. So you have no obstacle to being conscious of your responsibilities. You observe the facts of the self's life without judgment. You are open to help and solutions.

*Delilah realized that her need for status drove her into debt. With Truth in her awareness she is able to look at this without condemning herself. She recognizes that she had been confusing status with love. This was not wrong or bad. It was simply misguided. She goes to a financial counselor and works out a plan to pay off her debt.*

*Bob's son, Leo, is a manipulative sociopath. For most of Leo's life guilt drove Bob to enable his son in his manipulations. But without guilt in his mind Bob is able to accept Leo as he is and to build boundaries to keep Leo from disrupting his life.*

As you cease to believe in guilt you are willing to be conscious of and to release your projections of absolute-moral meaning. You no longer feel like a victim of a cruel world.

*Tess has grown her awareness of Truth and released much guilt. She has come to view her emotionally distant father not as a bad man but as a man trying to cope with guilt and fear just as she used to do. She no longer sees herself as his victim.*

*When Jeremy caught the news on television he would get upset. When he first became aware of Truth he was so easily charged that he had to avoid news programs like the plague. It seemed to him that the world had gotten worse. But he learned that it was just that he was looking directly at guilt instead of denying it. He also learned that the guilt that he saw in the world was his own belief in guilt. Now that he has worked out a lot of the guilt in his mind he is rarely charged if he sees a news story. And if he does experience a charge he releases it quickly by turning inward and remembering that only the Truth is true.*

Without guilt in your mind you do not have much use for a past or a future. The personal self's story of victimhood falls away. And its pleasant memories are no longer needed to offset present pain. You do not need to live in the future to escape present pain, either.

*Jane remembers that she used to blame her mother for much of her present pain. But now that Truth is true for her she cannot remember what it was that her mother was supposed to have done to her.*

*Since he has worked out much of the guilt in his mind Jonathan finds he does not fantasize about future happiness anymore. He lives fulfilled in the present with Truth.*

When the Truth is true for you and guilt is not, you find that you do not dwell on stories in the world. You live in the present and you are not tied to outcomes because they are not here now.

*Sally lives in the present with Truth. She reads books and the newspaper, she watches television and movies, but when she is done with them she does not give them much thought. They are all just to pass the time.*

*Dwayne listened to Rodney's long list of laments as he rested in Truth himself. He offered sympathy and gave advice when it was requested. In the following days he called to check up on Rodney and to offer further support. But he didn't give Rodney's problems much thought otherwise.*

When you live consciously in the present you are more aware of what is going on around the self. The self's life is more serendipitous, synchronous, and intuitive. So it is more harmonious.

*Louis caught the sound in his car's engine because he was mindfully present. He took his car to the shop as soon as he could. The mechanic told him that if the belt had fully busted it would've cost thousands more to fix the subsequent problems.*

*Monty has noticed that as he grows his awareness of Truth and lives more fully in the present every aspect of his life runs more smoothly. He anticipates problems or catches them early, knows intuitively when something needs to be done, finds answers and solutions faster, and sees connections between people and/or situations he knows he missed before.*

When you are present and conscious you are no longer baffled by your own motivations. You are aware when you feel an emotional charge and you address is quickly.

*Bess was angry when she heard the story about the dog being beaten. But she quickly realized that she was projecting absolute-moral meaning and making it real to herself. She turned her mind inward and remembered that only the Truth is true. She released what she realized was a typical story of dysfunction in an imperfect world of people in pain.*

## 28. Releasing guilt and raising children

If you are raising children you may wonder how you can do so without reinforcing guilt in their minds. Every self is born into a consciousness of guilt and fear. Guilt and fear is in the personal thought system in their mind. And the world around them reinforces guilt and fear. This is the experience of not-Truth. You will reinforce guilt, too, until you undo all of the guilt and fear in your mind. But remember that this is not wrong or bad. Do not add to your guilt. Your mistakes are opportunities to release guilt.
Children learn more from your energy and the attitudes that you model than from the words that you say. If you feel guilt they will pick up on it even if your words seem to indicate that you do not believe in guilt. Children will respect you more if you are honest. It is most important to not be hard on yourself. If you are self-forgiving they will learn the most valuable lesson from this. They will learn to forgive themselves. And that is all they really ever have to forgive.

You can model true forgiving for your children at any time, even if in the past you have been hard on yourself and/or them. It is healthy for them to see you willing to accept your mistakes, apologize, and make amends if necessary. They will learn to not turn their social conscience into guilt.

Because you want to be a good model for your children you can use your relationship with them to hold yourself accountable.

*Tatiana was about to spout off about the poor service that she was experiencing in the grocery store. But her son is with her and she catches herself. His presence reminds her that she does not want to look at the situation from the personal thought system. She takes a deep breath, relaxes, and centers her mind in Truth. She realizes that she is making a mountain out of a mole-hill. The poor service is not personal. The store is just poorly managed. This is not wrong or bad. It is just the way it is.*

Whether or not you raise children it is important to not be hard on yourself in the process of releasing guilt. Self-condemnation does not release guilt. It adds to guilt.

Since all of the guilt that you see comes from your belief in your own guilt, you must first be willing to release yourself from guilt. From there you will release your projections of guilt onto others. And when you have wholly released guilt only Truth and peace will remain in your mind.

## Acknowledgments

Thank you to Suzan Suits for proof-reading each of my books. I am, however, absolutely responsible for any errors in the final texts.

## About the Author

Liz Cronkhite is a life-coach and mentor who helps others release unconscious and conscious guilt. You can learn more about her and what she has to offer at www.lizcronkhite.net.

Made in the USA
Middletown, DE
09 August 2019